To Precious,
The journey
is worth the
sacrifice. God
will honor
you!

Journey
to
Wholeness

Immersion into a Bible-Based Life

Dr. John E. Guns

iUniverse, Inc.
Bloomington

Journey to Wholeness
Immersion into a Bible-Based Life

Copyright © 2011 Dr. John E. Guns

iUniverse books may be ordered through booksellers or by contacting:

iUniverse
1663 Liberty Drive
Bloomington, IN 47403
www.iuniverse.com
1-800-Authors (1-800-288-4677)

ISBN: 978-1-4620-1479-8 (pbk)
ISBN: 978-1-4620-1480-4 (cloth)
ISBN: 978-1-4620-1481-1 (ebk)

Printed in the United States of America

iUniverse rev. date: 06/03/2011

INTRODUCTION

As a youngster, I can remember vividly my mother referring to life as a "journey." This constant reference has become my foundation as I live out my life. Life is not simply a series of events and occurrences that have no connection. In fact, it is just the opposite. God has designed life as movement from place to place or moment to moment, and each place and each moment serves as an instrument of God to usher us into clarity regarding whom He is and who we are. As we begin to open ourselves to God, by allowing each place and moment to teach us, we will discover our destinations, our journeys.

Our individual destinations are not necessarily places; they are deeper understandings of our connections to God. It is about self-discovery. Note, however, that this self-discovery is not grounded in humanism but rather in who God has revealed Himself to be, supremely through Jesus Christ. Thus, our discoveries come as we live faithfully to the teachings of Jesus Christ and apply them to both the private and public areas of our lives.

As you embark on your journey, the goal is your wholeness. What is wholeness? It is a condition of a healthy and functional life grounded in the Word of God. It is about God and God alone. When you discover and experience wholeness, you then avail yourself fully to God and choose to live a committed life as a disciple of Jesus Christ. Wholeness is in and of itself a journey, and the person who desires it will find each day filled with new lessons. Each season of life will be filled with awe-striking revelations that push you into new and wonderful places with God. Each revelation will cause you to see yourself differently. They will allow you to explore the deeper dimensions of faith and walk away from each moment more passionate about the journey God has ordained for you.

Experience the thoughts and insights of me and others who feel a calling to share their journeys and who are committed to helping others fully comprehend God's grace and love. You will be **amazed as you** travel from place to place and moment to moment, **falling deeper in** love with God and growing to trust His Son, **Jesus Christ.**

This book is focused on devoting yourself entirely to God. No half-stepping, no trimming around the edges, just immersing yourself in His Word to hear His voice and changing the crazy way we all live by releasing all the negatives and replacing it with positives.

This is not a devotional but an *immersion*; it is an immersion because the goal is to have a daily focus on building your relationship with God. It is said that in order to learn a language as an adult, it's best to totally immerse yourself in the language and culture. Likewise, to develop a better relationship with God, you must totally immerse yourself in Him on this journey to wholeness.

Are you ready?

Here we go! Your journey to wholeness begins right now! It's going to be an awesome ride!

BE AT YOUR BEST

When I was younger, my mother used to say to me, "John, be at your best because you don't know what God has for you." Being at your best is about living each day governed by the standard of God and having the discipline to govern and place constraints on your conduct and conversations. God has entrusted you with much and each day is an opportunity to exhibit His glory to the earth. We each have a personal assignment that God has given us and we must set our goals to be at our best daily. Remember that God grants us grace each and every day. Grace empowers us to walk boldly as creative conquerors and refuse to settle.

I am excited! The world is aching for people who will rise to the top to put forth the awesome power of God. *I challenge you to be at your best.*

WORDS OF WISDOM:

- If you are working, give your best performance today.
- Have the best attitude you can have today.
- Discipline your conversations.
- Make a difference in someone's life.
- Be courteous, kind, and compassionate to family, friends, and strangers.
- Look for a moment to worship and keep God before you.

"God is waiting to open new and exciting doors but he needs you at your best."

Read: 1 Kings 10:1–13

YOUR THOUGHTS:

NO MORE DRAMA

One Sunday, I was sitting in a service in Houston, Texas and I noticed an interesting banner in the corner of the sanctuary. It was small and rather unobtrusive, but its message registered with me. It stated simply, *"2008: No More Drama."* As I prepared to preach, I found myself still riveted for a moment by the message. No more drama!

Once service was over, I began to think of the meaning of that statement. We all know about drama and have experienced it in one form or another. Drama is undue pain, discomfort, or suffering that clutters our personal spaces with confusion and disorder. We look for peace and calm only to discover that the drama has a seemingly lasting impact. I continued to pursue my thoughts on the subject. No more drama ... sounds good, but is it possible to fully experience a life without drama? For some of us, dramatic moments are the result of others' mismanagement of our spaces. Their choices and their unwillingness to do it right cause us unnecessary trepidation and fear. Of course, there are other dramatic moments that are simply results of old reliable us. We do things that are clearly not God's will, pressing forward with great confidence that there will be no fallout ... In the end; we experience pain and regrets for our choices.

How we deal with drama, whether it's the result of our doing or the result of someone else's decisions, defines us and carries us forward.

WORDS OF WISDOM:

- Turn to God for wisdom and direction.
- Confront the culprit of the drama, whoever it may be. Do so with the goal of resolution.
- Have the courage to do what must be done to restore order to your life. Your desire is to wake up every day with a sense of peace and an assurance of God's presence.
- Focus on what causes you peace, not what causes you pain. Often, your source of pain is in your immediate space; therefore, it is often a challenge to recognize its causes. Pay attention to the type of music you listen to, the content of

your conversations, and the books you read. You will be
amazed at their importance.
- Trust in the process of cleaning up your space, despite
  the pain you may experience. The end result is peace and
  comfort.

*"Enjoy life! Seek places of peace and strength. Seize this season. No more
drama!"*

Read: Psalms 23, 44; Ephesians 4:29; 1 Peter 5:5–7

YOUR THOUGHTS:

LOVE IT

I love what I do and I love where I am! Declare it and feel the excitement. Every morning when I wake up, I must admit my day is filled with an abundance of positives because of whom God has made me and where He is allowing me to go. It is amazing how incredible life becomes when you can access the mind of God for your purpose and destiny and with great conviction, commit your life's energy and attention to it. God so wants every one of us to wake up every day within the parameters of His purpose. This is where life is fun! Within the constraints of His will, you will discover the real meaning of favor and grace. I am so encouraged, knowing that all challenges and all battles are within the arena of God's awesome presence. All we have to do is choose Him and pursue Him with passionate intent.

WORDS OF WISDOM:

- Isolate the positive thoughts in your mind, and feed them with attention and activity.
- Enjoy people who enjoy you! Someone out there loves being with you! Find them, and enjoy the experience of giving and receiving love.
- Try something that makes you stretch.
- Develop a spirit of appreciation. Learn to nurture what matters to you.
- Finally, celebrate God's grace through Jesus Christ. Thank God daily for your second chance at life.

"Life is meant to be enjoyed. Love who God is making you and love what God has you doing at the present. Give it your best. Make today, tomorrow, next week, next month, next year, and the next decade your best yet. Donald Lawrence says it best: "You ain't seen nothing yet!"

Read: 2 Corinthians 4:1-12; Ephesians 2:10

YOUR THOUGHTS:

GOOD MORNING

Every morning my dog, Angel, awakens and begins her daily ritual. She comes to the edge of the bed and begins her attempts at licking me awake. For some of you this might appear slightly disgusting, but it is Angel's way of saying, "Good morning. I need to go outside."

Thinking about Angel's daily ritual made me think about something: How do we say good morning? How do we begin each new day with all its possibilities? How do we greet others in our spaces? How do we respond to a good morning extended to us?

It is important to realize that the way we begin our mornings defines the rest of the day. If we wake up and half speak (barely open our mouths to say anything), then that has an intricate influence on our day. Our morning attitudes, toward both those in our homes or toward our co-workers, are important.

WORDS OF WISDOM:

- Make a to-do list for your new good morning routine.
- Give yourself five minutes before getting up. Use this time to gather yourself and embrace the joy of a new day.
- See the first good morning as the first fruit of your day.
- Embrace your morning greetings with joy at home, at work, or wherever you happen to be.
- Make sure you spend quality time with God; allow Him to shape your morning.
- Practice until it becomes habit.

"Good mornings are a part of our foundations. Take a page out of Angel's book and learn to be pleasant and positive each morning."

Read: Colossians 3:12-17; Proverbs 17:22

YOUR THOUGHTS:

NOTHING LIKE GOOD FRIENDS

There are many experiences that make life enjoyable. One of the most important is relationships. A good relationship is more precious than anything in the world. Having great friends who walk with you through thick and thin is invaluable. I have found that true friends are those who are rigid enough to not let you destroy yourself and flexible enough to manage your moments of growth. Friends absorb your weaknesses and expose your strengths. They push you to fly when you want to walk. They help you sing when you want to cry.

To have a good friend also means you have to be a good friend; you have to put in the time and effort that goes into maintaining the relationship. It might appear easier to just say, "I don't need any friends," for fear or an unwillingness to put in the work required. However, I strongly believe that no one who claims a relationship with Jesus Christ should go through life friendless. We must be willing to put in the work. Just the fact that we embody and embrace the spirit of Christ makes us attractive to others; it shows patience, tolerance, kindness, forgiveness, and humbleness. All these qualities help others relate to us.

I encourage you to be the kind of person that makes friendship easy. Be a person who loves and lives well. This means that for all you do, make sure you continuously work on you so that you are attracting good friends.

WORDS OF WISDOM:

- Make yourself friendly.
- Learn to smile and laugh more.
- Make every effort to speak life to those you love.
- Work at being tolerant and patient with others.
- Stay away from sarcastic conversation and cynical tones.
- Develop the ability to be a pleasant person.

"Today, make yourself friendly and watch how God will wed a "Jonathan to your David." Have a friendly filled day."

Read: 1 Samuel 20:3–4; John 15:15–16

YOUR THOUGHTS:

WATCH YOUR WORDS

As I was on a plane one day, I sat under an amazing conviction as the Lord challenged me to become a better steward of my words. God led me to read James 3:9 and asked me, "John, if you love Me so much, why is it that your conversation, as it relates to others, does not always reflect My love?" He showed me in the Word a transforming revelation of how a person with a tongue that honors God can dishonor those God has created in His own likeness. This means that my positive speeches about God (we call it worship) is negated by my negative speech about what God loves and chooses to create in His own likeness. In essence, for all my God talk, I adversely affect it by employing negative and menacing words and comments about my family, my friends, and yes, even my enemies. It was a tough revelation to swallow as it called me to greater accountability in an area that sometimes seems so out of control.

Many of us find that our tongues have too much authority. Our tongues attack with no regard. Our tongues question the integrity of others with no sense of discipline. Our tongues destroy and look around like "who me?" when confronted with their own hate. God, who loves us so, is thus deeply bothered that we are often so causal and callous with our words. Families are offended, friends are wounded and enemies are strangely confirmed as a result of our failure to discipline ourselves in this area.

What a plane ride! I felt awful and yet, at the same time, so grateful that God would love me enough to call me into greater accountability. Now, I call you into the same accountability. God is calling you to have a greater respect for Him by having a more disciplined approach to how you speak of others.

WORDS OF WISDOM:

- "Live out the Will of God through your conversations."
- "Properly frame your words to worship God and speak life."

"It is time to watch your words."

Read: Proverbs 15:1; Ephesians 4:29; James 3:1–10

YOUR THOUGHTS:

GOD WILL MEET YOU IN THE GARDEN

What are you planning to plant in your garden of life today? This is such an awesome question. Notice, I did not ask what you are *planting* today. Rather, I asked what you are *planning* to plant today. God has granted you the authority and the ability to determine what you will plant today.

Planting is about the intentional release of that which produces what you desire. Planting is powerful; it provides you with the ability to decide what you believe you will bring to pass as God's outcome. Your belief in what God has ordained for you is the key. If I believe God has ordained great relationships for you, you cannot then haphazardly treat people any way and expect to receive His harvest of great relationships. Only plant what produces great relationships. If you desire a certain quality of relationship, intentionally do certain things to produce that quality. Planting empowers you as you become consciously intentional in all your behavior.

Are you encouraged today to synchronize your planting with God's standard? Are you encouraged to do what produces what you desire? This is a perfect day to live out God's standard for you by doing intentional things. No more wanting it to get better. Direct your day and your life according to what God says is possible. As we know and as your actions will prove, with God all things are possible.

WORDS OF WISDOM:

- Plant until it changes and then change because you planted.
- Embrace new growth and fresh opportunities.

"This day is going to bless you because within it is the chance to do awesome things by intentionally behaving and giving according to God's revealed standard for your life."

Read: Ecclesiastes 11:4; Galatians 6:7–10

YOUR THOUGHTS:

TRUST GOD TODAY

I woke up one morning and heard the words, "Trust God today." Immediately I asked the question, "Trust God to do …?" Yet at the end, it was clear: just trust God today. This was God's way of centering me to have the kind of day He wanted me to have.

Often when we wake up, we are so distracted by our morning routines that we neglect to center ourselves appropriately. *Trust God today* was not a warning that something was coming; rather it was a reminder of how to productively handle every day. This is such an important declaration for men and women of faith. Trusting God is foundational to everything we claim is God's will for us. Begin each day with the simple declaration that you will trust God today.

How do you strengthen your trust and confidence in God? It is simple!

WORDS OF WISDOM:

- Read the Word of God consistently so that your faith will be matured.
- Develop a morning routine that includes reflection, journaling, and prayer.
- Take faith breaks midday and reenergize your faith in a quiet moment with God.
- End the day with a time of cleansing worship, and become fully centered in God.

"Listen, sons and daughters, each day bring its challenges. The only way to victoriously win is to trust God today."

Read: Proverbs 3:5–5; Romans 10:17; James 1:19–25

S# 14   Sep.16'11 (Fri) 22:27

KVS Order 23

QTY	ITEM	TOTAL
2	FRUIT & WALNUT SALAD	3.78

Subtotal	3.78
Tax	0.28
Take-Out Total	4.06

Cash Tendered	20.06
Change	16.00

MCDONALDS # 2971

YOUR THOUGHTS:

THE POWER OF THANK YOU

There are two words, when partnered, have an impact so amazing that it is immediately felt. These two words form an unique ministry team. These two words are *thank you*. It is amazing to watch the results when *thank you* is sincerely uttered. These two words turn tense moments into pure pleasure. They are capable of transforming frowns into smiles. *Thank you* changes your context almost immediately into a spirit of gratitude and appreciation.

I have come to understand the power of *thank you*, and because of that I have come to value it. *Thank you* serves as the foundation of your personal and corporate worship. It allows you to move beyond a selfish moment to an acknowledged moment of obvious appreciation. I cannot deny the challenge I feel at times to utter it. When life is complicated by failure and frustration, *thank you* seems irrelevant. When life is invaded by pain and insufficiency, *thank you* is often difficult to say. Yet when declared out of a sincere heart, *thank you* empowers you to see the good in every moment.

You may ask, "Pastor, why do you believe this?" I believe this because I have seen this simple declaration turn a situation around. As powerful as *I'm sorry* is, *thank you* is just as powerful. Finding the humility to express to others how appreciative you are, even for the simplest act, makes an incredible statement about you as a person. It exposes the purity and genuineness of your heart and allows you to move beyond a place of disconnection with others.

WORDS OF WISDOM:

- Begin each day with a thank-you to God.
- Throughout the course of the day, find both time and opportunity to share your appreciation.
- This is a perfect day to use the ministry of thank you.
- *"Be amazed at how the power of "thank you" affects you and those with whom you share it."*

Read: Psalm 34:1–4; Philippians 4:7–8

YOUR THOUGHTS:

SUNDAY IS COMING

Every morning after her morning ritual, Angel, the "first dog", wakes up and runs to the patio doors. She sits there, anticipating when the doors will open and she will be free to run outside. She also sits patiently as she waits to be fed. After the food is prepared and placed in her food tray, she eats with pleasure.

I thought about this as it relates to the Word of God and believers. Each of us who claims to love God should be just as excited and just as hungry as Angel. What does this mean? It means that on Sunday, the tray (preaching) is filled with food (the Word of God) and you are given the opportunity to eat. Eating has to do with hearing the Word of God and then looking for ways to apply it. It has to do with desiring the Word and taking advantage of every opportunity God provides for us to hear the Word of God. It is so important in this season of your life that you sit with great anticipation as it relates to the Word of God. You need to be hungry, and that means just as Angel cannot wait to eat, likewise you are just as eager to hear what God has to say.

WORDS OF WISDOM:

Through the Word of God:
- Your faith grows
- You come to fully know the will of God for your life
- You understand God's expectations for you
- You confidently declare God's thoughts to the world

"The Word of God must become your passion in order to help you grow and develop. As one of my favorite professors, Dr. Jerome Ross, would say each Friday when I was a student at Virginia Union, "Sunday is coming and gotta preach! Sunday is coming, so get ready to grow!"

Read: Mark 4:1–20; James 1:19–26

YOUR THOUGHTS:

DREAMS DO COME TRUE

I am a firm believer that dreams come true. The dream is God's uniquely crafted purpose and plan for your life. It is God's undeniable call to greatness and your willingness to pursue it with all that is within you. I find it so important to fully embrace this dream and allow God to guide you through the challenges and processes until its arrival occurs. Arrival is dream fulfillment. It is an awesome place because now all that you have endured and sacrificed makes sense. Your life now comes together, and God allows you to enter into this incredible place of knowing that Romans 8:26–28 rings true.

Dreams can come true and God desires you to see the day when all you have sacrificed for manifests itself. God wants that for you in this lifetime. Let God allow you to see the wonderment of dream fulfillment.

At this moment, you are in the pursuit of a dream. Many dreams have been realized; however, some are still in various stages of development. Your personal passion rings true and if you have passion, you will see God at work.

WORDS OF WISDOM:

- Pray! Stay connected to the dream through your relationship with God.
- Partner. Partner through fellowship with other dreamers.
- Persevere. Never become discouraged.

"Go after the dream that defines who you are in God because dreams with God really do come true."

Read: Jeremiah 29:11; Romans 8:26–28

YOUR THOUGHTS:

GUARD YOUR MIND, OPEN YOUR HEART

Once again, I was sitting alone one day when God said to me, "Guard your mind and open your heart." I was in awe as His statement took me by storm. How could I possibly do this? I mean, people can hurt me, and by exposing myself, I allow negative emotions into my space. On the other hand, in order to learn and grow, one has to keep an open mind. I tried to convince myself that maybe I had heard God wrong, yet I knew I had heard Him right. It finally dawned on me: God wants me to guard my mind and open my heart in relation to Him and others.

When it relates to others, be careful that you protect who and what influences your thoughts. Guard your conversations, and direct their content toward your destiny and your growth. Know your limits. Refuse to give space to what you know will work against your growth and development. Couple that with an open heart for God, and know that through worship, He will grow and nurture you to become a person living fully and completely. Always keep your heart open to God, who cares for you unconditionally.

WORDS OF WISDOM:

- I challenge you to guard your mind and constantly stay open to God. You will be amazed at your incredible journey.
- God allows you to feel loved and affirmed and moves you beyond the uncertainties that accompany life.

"Enjoy God, who has, through Jesus Christ, offered Himself and continues to do so."

Read: Philippians 4:6–8

YOUR THOUGHTS:

STAY HUNGRY

Have you ever been hungry for a particular meal and nothing else could curb your appetite? That's how God wants you to feel about your life. He wants you to *stay hungry*, hungry for your dreams, your hopes, and your desires.

To stay hungry means you passionately go after life and refuse to allow anything to discourage you into inactivity. The experience is awesome. Staying hungry allows you to accomplish all that God has for you. It allows you to never settle or become so comfortable with your present place that you fail to go after life. This is the key to *staying hungry*.

WORDS OF WISDOM:

- God has so much life in you.
- Refuse to die before you fully live.

"Again, stay hungry and see how good it is when you begin to take a bite out of your life."

Read: Joshua 1:1–10; Philippians 3:14

YOUR THOUGHTS:

YOU ARE DISMISSED

Do you have anyone in your space that has hurt you so badly that forgiveness is a challenge? Are you presently living with the pain of unresolved issues that continue to dog you? Are you finding it difficult to let someone who disappointed you be released from the burden of your pain? If so, today is a great day to dismiss them from that place in your life through forgiveness.

It sounds strange, but forgiveness allows you to release those who have hurt you and those that have let you down. Forgiveness is authentically treating others as Jesus Christ would. Do you remember how He dealt with those who hurt Him? On Calvary, he dismisses us from the weight of our failure by forgiving us.

I understand how painfully weighty unforgiveness is. I understand how much it takes away from you, but I also understand how liberating and healing forgiveness is. I understand how powerful it is to walk away from a hurting season with a healed heart. Forgiveness is your weapon against the demonic tool of offense. God provides us with the strength to forgive and the ability to love again.

WORDS OF WISDOM:

- Identify the damage unforgiveness has caused you, and limit it through your prayer time.
- Embrace the grace of God, and then allow it to be extended to others through you.
- Pray your way through it.
- Dismiss others from the place of unforgiveness, and know you are stronger because of it.

"Choose to forgive because through it God liberates you to experience the tomorrow you're created for."

Read: Luke 6:27–36, 23:26–3

YOUR THOUGHTS:

THIS TOO SHALL PASS

One afternoon it was raining very hard, accompanied by thunder and lightning. While driving home, I found myself on the defense as I concentrated on the dangerous and wet roads. The rain seemed like it would never end. Instead of slacking up, it intensified. As the landscape began to flood, I questioned if the rain would ever end. In that moment, the rain began to lessen. I was amazed at how quickly it happened. In that moment, a very important spiritual lesson was reaffirmed for me: no matter what we go through, it all passes or ends eventually.

One of the challenges of life is believing that what we are going through will eventually end. It is holding to the conviction that God is a God who remembers where we are and, in His time, brings us out. How important this belief is to hold firm to! God loves us, and though we go through tough seasons and painful moments, He honors us by bringing us through. He brings us through by placing others in our lives who have either been through what we are going through or who encourage us while we are in the midst of our suffering.

WORDS OF WISDOM:

- God also releases us to His Word; that Word speaks to where we are and where we are going.
- It is important to know that whatever season you are in, God speaks confidently to you, which allows you to walk confidently in Him, with no fear of failure.

"Today go forth in the assurance that even in your current place, "This too shall pass."

Read: Psalms 23, 34:1–8; John 16:33

YOUR THOUGHTS:

DREAM DEFENDER

One of the great challenges of life is willingly fighting for your dreams. I recently had a conversation with an extremely gifted person. His dream is so incredible, and when achieved, it will have a tremendously positive impact on his industry. However, this gifted person is in a season—a season of fighting through what appears to be obvious limitations. When I talked to this person in turmoil, it was apparent to me that the only thing he lacks is the confidence to follow his dream in a season of challenges.

The reality is that dream fulfillment is the result of passion, confidence, and a profound sense of fearlessness all coming together in the same season. The dream happens because you believe so deeply in what God has called you to do that you fight through the season when it appears or it will not come to pass. Through Jesus Christ, God empowers you and keeps you moving forward. His Word energizes you daily, and you find yourself protecting the vision God has for your life. Your dream becomes something worth defending and protecting. It becomes something that you know must be accomplished; otherwise, God will not be pleased. You and the fulfillment of your dreams are one of the keys to making the world better. The courage to fulfill your goal and the need to succeed is crucial.

WORDS OF WISDOM:

- Read material that keeps you centered, especially the Bible.
- Choose a time each week to work on your dream. Do something focused exclusively on your dream.
- Keep your dreams on your prayer list. Seek God for wisdom, direction, resources, and relationships as you work toward accomplishing your goal.

"I challenge you to become your very own personal dream defender. Courageously face your limits, and push through them. You deserve to see your dream come to pass!"

Read: Jeremiah 29:11; Philippians 4:19

YOUR THOUGHTS:

NOT A BAD JOURNEY AT ALL

I had a revelation one day that brought clarity to my own journey. Though my path has taken some seemingly strange and painful routes, each step has been necessary to produce the person I am becoming. I found myself appreciating God for affirming my journey.

I write this because many of you are like me. Your journey has not been the most direct route; however, each step has been necessary. At times, the pace of God and the path He has carved seems so painful and tedious until you wonder if God is even there. Yet there is good news; all you have gone through has produced the person God honors now. What an exciting view of your life! God has ordered your steps, and no matter how much you want the easier path, God has determined that path with outcome in mind.

WORDS OF WISDOM:

- Nurture your faith through a disciplined reading of the Word of God.
- Look for God in all you go through. This involves shaping your views around the spirit of optimism.
- Connect to people who see their journeys as processes of God's will and not individual moments of disconnection.

"My friends, God has your life, and even if you have to take what seems to be the long way, trust God. You will be amazed at how incredible your journey is. Enjoy the ride!"

Read: James 1:2–3

YOUR THOUGHTS:

DECLARE IT TODAY

There is a very simple message I would like to share with you: God is in charge. This message is comforting, especially in light of all we face and must go through. God is truly in charge. Find solace and security in the fact that no matter what you face, God is in charge. He protects and preserves you! He guards you by guiding you. His hand covers you, and no matter what life brings, He never relinquishes control of your destiny.

WORDS OF WISDOM:

- Today is a great day to walk in the assurance that God is in charge. Know it, confess it, embrace it, and finally, rest in it.
- Daily declare that God has you and that you cannot and will not fail. Rest assured that all things truly are working for your good and that in God, you are protected.

"Be excited about today and the days to come because God is in charge and others, at best, are partners in your promotion."

Read: Psalm 23; Proverbs 3:5-6

YOUR THOUGHTS:

IT'S MONDAY

I have a personal philosophy that wakes up with me every Monday: Monday begins the process. While most churches are closed on Mondays, Saint Paul, the church I pastor in Jacksonville Florida, is open. I believe Monday is the most important day of the week. Mondays begin the process of the week, and a great start will translate into a great finish. For me, of course, the finish comes on Sunday morning.

When my Monday begins rested, focused, excited, and centered, I find the week better. With my Sundays spent in the presence of God, beginning the process right provides the perfect balance for the week.

Properly manage your week by appropriately seeing and approaching Mondays. With that said, I share with you advice to manage your Mondays.

WORDS OF WISDOM:

- Choose a verse or passage to engage in devotional reading for the week, and begin your week with a time of intense prayer.
- Journal your desire for the week, and review your desire each day. Believe me, this will aid greatly in maintaining your focus.
- Rise early on Monday and "quiet" the morning by meditating on how you desire your week to look.
- Create your to-do list on Sunday night. Monday, reflect on what you need to accomplish.

"Monday is very important. Enjoy it, and remember that God has the plan for you. Give him your ear. Be blessed."

Read: James 4:10

YOUR THOUGHTS:

I CHALLENGE YOU

God challenged me, and so I am challenging you. I challenge you to courageously conform to the image of Christ, who has called you out of darkness. I challenge you to align your mindset with the vision God has for you. I challenge you to correct yourself in the areas where you are weak and inconsistent. I challenge you to move beyond protecting what can disconnect you from divine favor and purpose. Want God and His favor more? Know then that anything that disrupts your relationship with God is not worth it. Remember Samson. Remember Saul. Remember Judas. Know that to lose access to God's grace and purpose is too costly of a price. Embrace your call and your destiny, and at the same time, coordinate your conduct with the standard of your destiny and call.

WORDS OF WISDOM:

- I challenge you to let nothing cause you to downsize your life.

"Be blessed!"

Read: Proverbs 11:31, 16:1–3; Colossians 3:12–17

YOUR THOUGHTS:

DON'T SETTLE

Have you ever commissioned someone to do work for you or have you ever purchased something only to discover its quality does not suit you? In that moment, you find yourself with the dilemma of either accepting what has been presented to you or exposing the gaps between your expectation and reality. In the end, you require your expectation because you do not see it as unrealistic.

This is the same attitude you should carry into all aspects of life. Regardless of what you face and where you are, God has deposited in you a standard. This standard is sometimes difficult to communicate; though you are clear about what it is not, you are not always clear about what it is. You know that it is better than what has been presented to you.

This is equally, if not more, true about the quality of your relationships. You have an internal standard that God has deposited in you. This internal standard is specifically related to the type of relationships that fit your destiny. God exposes you to this standard in some way and requires you to go after it. God warns you in various ways when it comes to whom you should relate and how relating to that person will affect your future. Yet far too often, settling is the easier path.

You allow people to bring clutter into your life with their latest issues. You give people permission to disrespect you with their mismanagement of loyalty and honesty, thus empowering them to disregard you. Most importantly, they do not feed you what is needed for your destiny.

WORDS OF WISDOM:

- Don't settle, embrace God's standard for you.
- Decide that God knows best. If you are uncomfortable with something, voice your standard and trust it.
- Know that God has trusted you with this intrinsic sense, and confidently live in it. God loves you!

"Have an awesome, standard-guided day!"

Read: John 15:11–17; Romans 12:9–21

YOUR THOUGHTS:

THANKS FOR THE PUSH

I was in Atlanta, preaching for one of my dearest friends. While my family and I spent time with his family, I found myself positively pushed by their lifestyle and standard. Not by just the house and cars, but by the excellence that clearly flowed from his life. In that moment, a profound sense of personal standard was resurrected in me. I understood the value of my life and the standard that I desire for my life again. It was a wonderful feeling to be called back to a place that I had at one time embraced and willingly claimed.

Understand that the emphasis of this devotional is not focused on buying things to validate you. The point is that you need friends who push you and challenge you without saying a word. The push is not about forcing something on you but about you fully embracing the *will* of God and allowing God to introduce you to your God-ordained level. This level, or standard, is intrinsic; it is buried under the murk of your reality. Sometimes reality becomes so controlling that you cease to walk in your standard. In those moments, God uses your friends to push you. Their elevation, their promotion, their purchase of a new home, their completion of school, or any of their other accomplishments send you into a place of serious reflection, causing you to rethink and forcing you to think clearly about life. In the end, your friends push you, and you are grateful for their presence.

Ask yourself these questions this morning:
(1) What kind of friends do I have, and do they reflect my desired standard?
(2) Are they an expression of my past, present or future?

WORDS OF WISDOM:

- I believe friends ought to reflect something about you and call you to greater levels of spirituality, morality, and accountability. God speaks through friends.

"I love you and have an incredible week."

Read: Proverbs 27:17; Ecclesiastes 4:9–12

YOUR THOUGHTS:

GOD DID A GREAT JOB

I woke up one morning on the beach in Fort Lauderdale, Florida, tired from an exhausting but awesome day of worship. My body was tired, my mind was in a little slow in operation, and my emotions drained, I opened the window *and wow*! It hit me. The sun was bright, the water was beautiful, the sand was white, and the waves swayed gently back and forth. In that moment of exhaustion, I had to admit to myself, God did a great job. I saw His creation and understood how caring and careful God was in creating the world. I further understood that God is not only the Creator but also the Sustainer of this vast creation and its system of operation. In that moment, I valued God even more. God, you did a great job!

What is so interesting to me is that there was a day when I did not appreciate or even notice creation. The demands of my life cluttered my view so much; I was consumed with me and mine. In those moments, I sat among God's handiwork and failed to fully appreciate it. I benefited from it, played in it, walked amongst it, but I was too concerned with me to say thank you to God. But life has a way of bringing you center and reminding you that life is bigger than you. In those times, seeing God as Creator and Sustainer is vital.

WORDS OF WISDOM:

- I encourage you to not become so consumed with the demands of this season of your life that you fail to celebrate and appreciate God as Creator.

"God really did do a great job! Have an incredible day!"

Read: Psalm 19

YOUR THOUGHTS:

ADDRESS THE CONTRADICTIONS

My first full day in Johannesburg birthed this revelation. As I woke to prepare for what I knew was going to be an amazing day, I heard so clearly the voice of the Lord declare to me, "Address the contradictions." The moment I heard it of course, I began to wrestle with what exactly that meant. Literally within moments of asking the question, the answer came back. Addressing the contradictions mean, "confronting traits, situations, relationships, and decisions that clearly go against the grain of what and who I have created you to be." It means facing the FACT that some of your life is unhealthy and it does not reflect who God has fashioned you to be. It means removing the irrelevant, the distracting, and the unnecessary. It involves knowing God's will for your life and all that your life should resemble and having the courage to live governed by clarity. The Lord said to me that my life at this stage should:

- Be drama free & simple
- Enjoyable & healthy
- Growth-oriented
- Increasing in every area

How about you? What is God calling your life to be? What will it take for you to arrive there? What major decisions do you need to make so God gets the most out of you? What minor adjustments do you need to do to insure that life will give back to you all God desires for you?

WORDS OF WISDOM:

- Don't let things linger that are clearly no longer in season for you.
- Notice the complications that come with people and situations and courageously confront them.
- Speak the Will of God to yourself daily.
- Give in to the Holy Spirit, fully embracing your spirituality as foundational to your life.

"Life is to be experienced, not avoided!"

Read: John 15:1-10

YOUR THOUGHTS:

WHO'S FEEDING YOU?

My daughter and I were in Fort Lauderdale, spending some daddy-daughter time together. While relaxing in the water, I noticed an interesting sight—a piece of seaweed floating close by. Curious, I reached down to pick it up only to discover a group of small fish feeding from it. I decided to put it down, and the fish quickly migrated back to it and continued to eat. I thought to myself, "*Who is feeding me?*"

Old folks used to say, "You can't eat at everybody's table." That is also true when it comes to what you are consuming to feed your spirit. It is very important that you are careful about who you allow to feed you, that is, who you allow to feed your spirit.

WORDS OF WISDOM:

- Take full advantage of the positive people, groups, and places God places in your path.
- Open yourself up to the possibility of growing.
- Be very selective about who you allow to feed you.
- Watch your spiritual diet, and guard your dinner invitations.
- Do not allow anyone or anything to negatively affect you.

"Enjoy the day, and know God has a special meal for you.
Keep eating the right things from the right people in the right places!"

Read: John 15:1–11

YOUR THOUGHTS:

INSULATING YOUR WORLD

What does it mean when you insulate something? Insulation is the act of covering or surrounding something for the sake of preventing or reducing what you do not desire to negatively affect it. Insulation, as most of us know, is used primarily in homes to limit either the loss of heat, air, or electricity or to reduce sound.

The Lord clearly spoke to me recently. He said, "Insulate your life with only positives." I thought long and hard about His meaning and decided to break down the tools needed to insulate one's life.

Insulating your life is a process of reconstructing and deconstructing your space. It involves changing who and what you are and redesigning what is within you. It is about making adjustments for an improved you, accepting the challenge to become a better person, and embracing a brighter future.

As we explore what it means to insulate your life with *positives*, let's focus on three key points: attitude, relationships, and habits.

WORDS OF WISDOM:

- Journal your thoughts.
- What are you being exposed to that influences who and what you are?

"My friends, how you see your life will go a long way in determining the quality of life you experience. God has more, think like it."

Read: Philippians 3:12–14

YOUR THOUGHTS:

53

INSULATING YOUR WORLD WITH
THE RIGHT ATTITUDE

According to W.W. Ziege,"*Nothing can stop the man with the right mental attitude from achieving his goal; nothing on earth can help the man with the wrong mental attitude.*" This famous quote sums up the Bible's declarations regarding how man thinks. The right attitude is an incredible ally for those who are committed to excellence and who genuinely believe they are created for greatness. You will never achieve what God has for you without being a person with a positive and healthy attitude.

Insulating your life begins with your attitude. Your attitude consists of your thoughts, your disposition, and the way you manage your decision-making process. If you, with purpose, seek to have the right attitude, God will grant you all things in time.

WORDS OF WISDOM:

The right attitude is the result of the following:
- A healthy devotional life that centers you.
- A commitment to continued education that helps you grow.
- Intentional conversations with persons who operate with a positive attitude.

"Your attitude must align itself with God and His will for your life. My encouragement is that you take advantage of the growth opportunities before you and willingly allow your attitude to be shaped by God. Know that your attitude will always serve as an ally for your desired healthy, holy, and functional life."

Read: Proverbs 15:33, 19:8 & 25

YOUR THOUGHTS:

INSULATING YOUR WORLD WITH
THE RIGHT RELATIONSHIPS

Relationships are an instrument employed by God to develop you. He does not intend for you to live in this world successfully without relationships. Through relationships, God pushes you to new and exciting places, which shapes in you the ability to reflect His nature and the capacity to live in His image. Over the course of my forty-six years, I have experienced many relationships, and each has in some way aided my development. Whether positive or negative, each relationship in my life has participated in forming the man I am today.

Yet, I must admit that during difficult and lean years, I found relationships a nuisance and a bother. They seemed to cause more pain than pleasure. During that time, relationships often felt like the source of my discomfort and discontent. Now that I reflect on the past, I understand the purpose of that season of relationships was to expose something about me that God wanted addressed for greater glory. In the end, it was a good thing that I went through that season. Now, I understand that relationships are an ally, and I strive to have the kind of relationships that are a benefit to my destiny. That is my encouragement to you today. Experience relationships as God's instrument, and employ them to make you a better person.

WORDS OF WISDOM:

- As you mature, establish a non-negotiable standard for the kind of person you want in your life; define and separate the types of relationships in your life.
- Use the traits in Colossians 3:12–15 to evaluate yourself.
- Create an open spirit to allow you to comfortably say, "I am sorry"—three words that save relationships.

"Insulate your world through relationships. Honor God as you encounter others."

Read: Colossians 3:12–15

YOUR THOUGHTS:

INSULATING YOUR WORLD
WITH THE RIGHT HABITS

It has been stated that actions speak louder than words. When I say actions, I am referring to your habits. Habits are those things you do consistently and instinctively. Habits are reflections of the way you see yourself, and they make a clear statement about your priorities. It is important to note that one of the keys to insulating your world is through healthy, holy, and functional habits; in essence, doing the right behavior consistently until it positively affects everything around you. To stay positive and encouraging, you must develop the right habits, which requires discipline and accountability.

WORDS OF WISDOM:

- A daily devotional life that synergizes your focus on Jesus Christ.
- Open and healthy communication with those to whom you are committed.
- Exercise and healthy stress-relieving activity.
- Attendance to corporate worship experiences.
- Daily reading of the Bible.

"I want to encourage you to make a list of the attitudes, relationships, and habits you need to work on to help your life becomes positive from this point forward. Hold yourself accountable."

Read: Psalm 1; James 1:19–25

YOUR THOUGHTS:

I AM BETTER

Romans 8:28 declares that "all things" partner to produce a better person. This better person is someone that fully embraces Jesus Christ as Lord and continues to actively live out of faith despite their external situation. Promotion, then, is tied to how we manage those moments when we do not "like" them. God allows the moment because, in the end, it benefits us. In the mind of God, all life experiences have relevance. These experiences all come together to produce a person who is deeply passionate about their relationship with Jesus Christ and hungry to live a life worthy of the calling of God.

Promotion requires the journey. You must be willing to face each experience and situation courageously. This means that no matter how difficult the situation, God still has purpose tied to your pain. God loves you so deeply and with such great joy; He orders your steps. Even when He requires that you travel the long way and endure difficulties, God conforms it to the ultimate outcome—your life. Face life today knowing that everything will make you a better person.

WORDS OF WISDOM:

- Affirm your situation as being under the authority of God.
- Look first for the personal lesson, and then look for the lesson in others.
- Place the situation within your prayer time, and experience God in it.
- Journal the lessons you learn and apply them immediately to your life.

"Today is a great day to keep growing. Don't stop! *Keep growing! Know that all things are your allies toward promotion."*

Read: Romans 8:26–28; Colossians 3:17

YOUR THOUGHTS:

GAINING DIVINE FAVOR

What ultimately moves God's heart? If you wanted to impress God, what could or should you do? I know it sounds funny, but you can impress God. You can move the heart of God and cause the Eternal One to extend favor to you. God wants to honor and bless you. According to Jeremiah 29:11, He has designed your journey to arrive at a place of prosperity and increase. God declares in Proverbs 3:5–10 that He desires to direct your steps and honor you according to His abundant favor.

While reading one night, I asked of myself, "How can I experience greater divine favor?" God wants us to walk in the fullness of divine favor and experience *all* that He, through Jesus Christ, has ordained.

WORDS OF WISDOM:

A guide to gain divine favor:
- Uncompromising obedience (John 6:35–40)
- Generosity (2 Corinthians 9:6–15)
- Fearless faith (Matthew 15:21–28)
- Incredible devotion lived through worship (Psalm 34:1–8)

"God has so much for you and He wants you to walk in it. Today, model Jesus Christ, and watch God extend favor in an abundant way."

Read: Matthew 3:13–17

YOUR THOUGHTS:

THE STRESS OF PROMOTION

Pastor Arthur Jackson of Antioch Baptist Church in Carol City, Miami, preached an incredible word titled, "David's Anointing," taken from 2 Samuel 5:1–3. From the message came many lessons about promotion. One lesson that followed me to my morning devotional was a point he made about the problems that come with being anointed.

As he preached, I heard over and over again, "John, promotion brings increased stress." This stress is about God placing greater demand on you and requiring greater accountability. The demands of promotion increase the weight of your life as you find yourself placed in situations in which you are responsible for more and more. The job promotion to supervisor makes you responsible for employees who were your friends and are now your employees. The purchase of a larger home requires increased costs in electricity and water, additional expenses not felt with an apartment. The presence of a new relationship demands sacrifices and unselfishness not required when it was just you. Amazing, isn't it? In each situation, it was all easier before, but the rewards were definitely not the same.

WORDS OF WISDOM:

- Increase your prayer time. Only through the strength of God can you manage the demand of promotion.
- Make sure you surround yourself with Christ-centered, confident, destiny-focused people.
- Read character-forming and conduct-transforming material. Refresh and renew your mind with positive literature.
- Develop and embrace habits that relieve stress without adding the weight of divine judgment.

"Today, embrace promotion as a joy, not a burden. In the end, the stress of promotion will not hurt you; it will strengthen you. Have an awesome day!"

Read 2: Samuel 5:1–3; John 14:11–14

YOUR THOUGHTS:

NO FEAR, GO FOR IT

On August 27, 2008, like many people I stayed up until 2:30 AM watching the roll call and the speeches at the Democratic National Convention. As I listened to President Clinton and Senator Biden deliver powerful presentations, I was struck by the energy in the room. Then, a moment occurred that took the energy level in the Pepsi Center up a notch. Presidential nominee Barack Obama entered the room and joined Joseph Biden on stage. In that moment, it dawned on me: a black man had crossed a new threshold. It was such a powerful moment. I found myself sitting in the dark, simply watching, unable to move. What a memory!

This historic moment will always register to those of us who witnessed the occasion. I was overwhelmed. Here was a man who had faced insurmountable odds, attempting to achieve something that no one of color had ever achieved. It was a statement of his faith in Jesus Christ and his willingness to stretch out beyond what others had decided for him. How did he accomplish so much? The key is that Obama conquered fear and decided to move into the future despite the past facing him.

Just as David facing the giant, no doubt each of you have some call or some dream that continues to stand before you, behind the fear that you need to conquer. Moving past fear is about staring that which seems greater than you in the face, but not that which is greater than God. Move forward with the confidence you have in God.

WORDS OF WISDOM:

- Read the Word of God, and watch your faith grow. Read Romans 10:17
- Share your dream with people who have a strong faith and a deep passion for God. Read Romans 15:1-3
- Write down and embrace the dream. Read Habakkuk 2:1-4

"So, open the door, climb the mountain & fight the giant."

Read: I Samuel 17:41-51

YOUR THOUGHTS:

GOD, I AM READY

I decided to become more aggressive in declaring to God that I am ready. I am ready for so much more, and I am not the only one. God has created us to be great, and He has so much more for us. God has called us to walk in the more-than-enough place He wants for us more than we want for ourselves. We must position ourselves for God. My prayer is "God, I am ready."

WORDS OF WISDOM:

Tell God, I am ready for:
- Clarity for the next step;
- The evidence of God's favor in my life;
- Relationships that work for me and not against me;
- Manifestation of all your promises for my life.

Join me in this declaratory prayer today by saying, "God, I am ready!" and believe that God is ready as well. Have an awesome day!"

Read: Isaiah 61:5–9

YOUR THOUGHTS:

TIME TO BE WHOLE

In this season of your life, God desires to bring you into wholeness. Wholeness is about the removal of gaps and voids in your life. It is about existing in a place where you lack nothing because God has orchestrated a season of fullness. It is a powerful place because it is devoid of jealousy, envy, and unnecessary conflict. It is where God trusts you with more. Here, you experience a deep sense of peace and contentment. It is what Paul refers to in Philippians 4:11–13. I know God desires for you to walk in it.

WORDS OF WISDOM:

- Remove all unnecessary barriers to your peace of mind.
- Commit to working for peace.
- Deepen your personal worship by expanding the time you spend with God.
- Find peace and wholeness in Him.

"God desires you to be whole, so accept the challenge, and go after it."

Read: Philippians 4:11–13; Colossians 3:15

YOUR THOUGHTS:

GET OUT AND ENJOY

God and His Son, Jesus Christ, did an awesome job of creating this world. They created nature and all its amenities; family and friends who bring us great joy with their companionship; places of amusement where we can go for a moment out of our busy lives and simply be children again. They also created us to take walks, shop, eat, and laugh. Instead of being burdened with the cares of a busy and hectic schedule, take a moment and enjoy the world God has created.

Look around and decide that this day will be spent doing what makes you laugh. Talk to a friend you haven't talked to in a while. Take your favorite person someplace fun. Cheer on for your favorite team or sit and listen to your favorite music. God enjoys watching you take pleasure in what He has created.

WORDS OF WISDOM:

- Life can be tough, and sometimes your day has to be a no-stress day; a day for no arguing, no negative thinking, no cynical conversations, and no defeated behavior. This is a time to refresh!

"Know that God is secure enough to watch you enjoy life."

Read: Philippians 4:4–9

YOUR THOUGHTS:

ENCOURAGE YOURSELF

Ever had a day that seemed so overwhelming that you just wanted it to end? Just wanted to just push stop and start over? Do you remember when you were a child on the playground? If the game didn't go the way you liked, you could stop and ask for a do over. This day is like that. Everything is going against you. In the course of it all happening, you wait for someone to say or do something that will remind you of God's love for you. Yet feelings of hopelessness mount as the day becomes more and more challenging.

What do you do? Follow the example of David in 1 Samuel 30:6. David was placed in overwhelming conditions, and he found courage and strength in God. He used God's strength as encouragement. What a powerful portrait!

WORDS OF WISDOM:

- David centered on God and removed the distractions around him.
- David redirected his energy through worship.
- I advise you to decide to obey God and follow the Word of God.

"Learn to encourage yourself. Learn through prayer and meditation to remind yourself who you are in God and how incredible your God is. Remember, when no one else encourages you, find strength in God and encourage yourself."

Read: I Samuel 30; Acts 16:25–26

YOUR THOUGHTS:

MAKE YOUR MOUTH A MINISTRY

The old adage, "Sticks and stones may break my bones, but words will never hurt me," is a bold-faced lie. Words have power and carry a mighty swing. In the past, I have been guilty of using words as weapons to hurt and damage people, especially the people I love. My words have worked as an enemy, not an ally, to God's will. I now place great emphasis on my words serving as ministry, especially within my personal space.

In our public lives, many of us are careful of what we say. As my mother says, we temper our words. We carefully select our communication to present the best us. When we are away from the spotlight of the public and we are with our loved ones, we say things that seem to contradict the very name of loved, as we call them. In the end, we wound those closest to us. We shine in our public lives, but our private spaces are filled with tension and anxiety. This is tied to the fact that in our personal shelters our mouths are not ministry; they are weapons. Thus, our words become bullets and not blessings. There is no magical format for successfully managing your words.

WORDS OF WISDOM:

These three steps are a great start on the path to using your words always in love:

- Discipline your tongue to work on what you say and how you say it.
- Protect your temple; what goes in is what will come out.
- Spend more time in the presence of God until you live sensitive to the Holy Spirit.

"Join me in getting better in the area of our mouths, words, and body language. The people who love you will be eternally grateful."

Read: Ephesians 4:29; James 3:1–13

YOUR THOUGHTS:

KEEP LIVING UNTIL …

As I sat on a plane headed to Dallas, I found myself living in a powerful moment of fulfillment.

I had made the trip in response to an invitation from Bishop T. D. Jakes of the Potters House in Dallas, Texas, but my fulfillment was not the invitation or who it was from. The fulfillment came from the reality of how faithful God is.

Years ago, the Lord promised some things in my life. As I sat on that plane to Dallas, I heard God say, "I promised you". The amazing thing is that God's promises sometimes appear to take such a long time. His promises seem to require so many challenges. If you are not careful, you will become discouraged. Time, if you let it, will rob you of the faith you need to believe in the season of planting and preparation. You will face so many challenges that you might wonder if you really heard God accurately.

The key is to keep living until God proves He is faithful to His word. I know, it sounds good, but be encouraged not to give up. Keep living until …

WORDS OF WISDOM:

- Surround yourself with people who speak life into you. While you are waiting on God's promises, know He will come through. You need people who believe in you and in His promises for your life.
- Deepen your personal worship. Know that worshiping keeps you focused on the God in the promises, not just the promises.
- Learn to enjoy the season of preparation. Know God is shaping you to get you ready for what He promised you.
- Fight through the depression and discouragement.

"Keep living until … Be blessed!"

Read: Isaiah 55:10–11; Philippians 3:12–14

YOUR THOUGHTS:

AN EXCELLENT LIFE

An excellent life produces an excellent life! An excellent life is about doing the right things at the right times and allowing your decisions and behaviors to be influenced by an innate desire for the best. It has to do with a passion to excel using your Christian faith as the guide and the pathway.

God challenges us to take seriously the standard that is within us and to strive to be excellent on another level. In the end, an excellent life produces an excellent life.

WORDS OF WISDOM:

- Embrace the innate standard that is God's will for your life.
- Begin to expose yourself to what you desire as your standard.
- Read God's word, and let it become a way of thinking.
- Cleanse your life of inferior conversations and relationships.
- Conquer the fear of pursuing God's standard for your life.

"Today God says, "Go after the excellent way. An excellent life produces an excellent life.
Live in excellence!"

Read: 1 Kings 10:1–16

YOUR THOUGHTS:

FAITH WORKS

Faith works if you work faith! This idea is so simple. Many of us claim and confess Jesus Christ's struggle. Often our faith is not as healthy as it should be or as strong as it could be. Think about it this way: if you do not exercise your muscles regularly, you become weak. Well, you have a faith muscle, and it is only as strong as you make it. The question to ask yourself is why your faith muscle is weak.

WORDS OF WISDOM:

- We don't read or meditate as we should.
- We don't speak as positively as we should.
- We allow faith-deficient persons to speak into our lives.
- We exhibit an inconsistent worship-life.

"It is so important that you have healthy and functional faith. Your faith will serve you in tough times. Through your faith, you will discern and understand the will of God while dealing with a season of uncertainty. Faith is the ally of every disciple of Jesus Christ; grow it, nurture it, and protect it. Have a strong faith-filled day!"

Read: Matthew 15:21--28; Romans 10:17

YOUR THOUGHTS:

TRUST GOD'S WORD

My encouragement today is that you grow in your appreciation of God's word. This means learning to value God and all He says to you through the teachings of His Son, Jesus Christ. I am a witness that His Word keeps and sustains those who seek His wisdom, guidance, and correction. It is important that you grow to trust God and His Word. Trusting His Word will cause you to operate in radical obedience, and you will be amazed at how God provides and protects.

WORDS OF WISDOM:

- Identify the responses or activities that you should engage in when it comes to the Word of God.

"Trust His Word! Seize the moment! Have an awesome day!"

Read: Psalms 119:9-16

YOUR THOUGHTS:

GUARD YOUR DESTINY

God speaks to you and tells you who you are in Him. God lets you in on the secret of your greatness and gives you permission to walk, to be all you can be. Then, He gives you one directive: "Guard your destiny!" What does this mean?

Simply put, it means make decisions in light of what God has said to you about you. Live as a person of purpose and destiny. Choose to trust God by making Him your all and all. In the end, you stand guard over your uniqueness and do what you must do to ensure that God is pleased with you.

WORDS OF WISDOM:

Samson was a man who:
- Allowed his personal passions to stand in the way of fulfilling his destiny;
- Gave away the secret of his anointing to someone who did not care about him;
- Negotiated his standard because he did not have the discipline to deny himself;
- Struggled to control his temper.

"I encourage you to know who you are in God. You are great; live like it!"

Read: Luke 4:1–13

YOUR THOUGHTS:

CHOOSE YOUR FRIENDS WISELY—PART I

Lucy Larcom says, "Every true friend is a glimpse of God." I encourage you to think about your life and the roles your friends play in it. List your three most important relationships and why they are important to you. Take time to pray about who is in your life and who should be in your life. Your friends are the key to your ability to begin and complete God's ordained plan for your journey to wholeness.

WORDS OF WISDOM:

- Pay attention to what you hear and see.
- Pray and ask God to help you be a better friend.
- Be open to new friends.

"Take time to journal your personal thoughts."

Read: Ecclesiastes 4:9–12

YOUR THOUGHTS:

CHOOSING FRIENDS WISELY—PART 2

Here is probably the most important question to ask yourself regarding friends: "What should I look for when choosing friends in this season of my journey?"

WORDS OF WISDOM:

- Determine your personal standard based upon God's will and assignment for your life. Refuse to negotiate.
- Openly communicate to new relationships what your standards are and trust that honesty will prevail. Understand that once you reach a certain level of maturity, dishonesty at the beginning of a relationship is a clear sign of personal immaturity.
- Be on guard when you notice behavior that is inconsistent with your communicated standard.
- Notice the way friends handle crisis and conflicts. You want people in your life who feel a deep sense of accountability, even in challenging seasons.
- Allow friends to share with you understanding of their own personal destiny. If you connect to someone who feels a calling in his or her life or has discovered his or her purpose, that person's standard will also help push you toward your destiny.

"Know that God wants the best for you and only through healthy relationships can certain things happen in your life."

Read: John 15:11–17

YOUR THOUGHTS:

ARE YOU GROWING?

I have an important question for you: "Are you growing?" Jesus Christ died for us, and with his death, He created for us the opportunity to become better people. Becoming a better person is about growing or improving in each area of your life. It is about submitting to the Holy Spirit, yielding to the voice of God, and willingly obeying the Word of God.

I am excited for you. In this stage of your development, you will discover how incredible God really is. This discovery comes as you open yourself to growing and willingly allow yourself to be shaped in the image of Jesus Christ. God has so much more for us, and only through our relationship with Jesus Christ can we be all we are capable of being.

WORDS OF WISDOM:

- Enhance your personal relationship with God through your devotional time and attendance to corporate worship.
- Read, read, and then read some more! Expand your mind, and grow your knowledge base.
- Through your prayer time, seek an honest assessment regarding how God sees you and what He is calling you to do.
- Create relationships with people who are growth-oriented and who are committed to personal development and excellence.
- Finally, trust your process. God has you on a pace to arrive somewhere. Trust it and do not panic simply because your process is slower or more challenging than someone else's. God knows what's best for you! Go for it and grow from it!

"Growing happens as a result of your being open and willing."

Read: Luke 2:52; Philippians 3:10–16

YOUR THOUGHTS:

LET IT GO

One of my favorite passages is Psalm 131. While reading it one day, I sensed the Lord calling me to *let it go*. It was an awkward moment. I felt ashamed. I knew God had grown tired of me carrying certain things and managing certain relationships in a manner that made them a burden. Letting it go is such a challenge because it means literally releasing others from their responsibility, while still maintaining a relationship with them. It means no longer allowing pain and rejection to manage your day. Even if you were wronged, it means no longer treating those that have wronged you as the villain. Letting go is about moving on in the power of grace and forgiveness, knowing that you are loved by God and affirmed by Jesus Christ.

Know that letting go is a process that can only be navigated with a deep desire to please God and live above the oppression of negative emotions. This process will take you through some ups and downs but at the end of this journey, you will arrive at a place of perfect peace and renewed hope.

WORDS OF WISDOM:

- Take it to God in prayer. Sincerely seek the Lord for guidance on forgiveness and resolution.
- Read scripture that empowers you to live in a place of completion and wholeness.
- When given an opportunity, talk it through with either the person or someone whose spirit you trust. Do not deal with someone who is gossipy; you need a spiritual presence.
- Develop the ability to think positive thoughts. According to Philippians 4:8, fill your mind with life-giving traits and ideals.
- Focus on the positive aspects of your life, beginning with your relationship with Jesus Christ.

"Let it go! Enjoy the next moment. God has so much more for you and it begins with letting it go!"

Read: Luke 23:26-34

YOUR THOUGHTS:

LESSONS FROM A WISE MAN

I am one blessed man. All my life I have been privy to the example of a true Godly man in and through my father, Frank Guns, Sr. When I was a child, my father served as pastor at Abyssinia Baptist Church in Virginia while also working at the United States Post Office. I watched him as he juggled two full-time positions, all the while maintaining his family. As I matured, I saw my father transition into full-time ministry and again, he showed strength and commitment and provided excellent leadership. Upon retirement, his assignment changed as my mother's health took a turn and she became a double amputee. I have watched him in his later years continue to exemplify strength and commitment as he cares for his wife of over sixty years. For me, my father has been an example of great strength and loyalty.

The lesson I have learned from my father is one of profound and unwavering commitment. Throughout his eighty-one years on this earth, he has overcome many obstacles to become an enduring and endeared leader among ministers throughout the state of Virginia. I have watched him love my mother while faithfully serving the people of God. How blessed I am.

I encourage all of you to understand that, in the end, a life is more than what you possess or purchase. Life is about your commitments and your willingness to follow them through. The lesson of my father is that when you say yes, you prove your worth by standing strong in your commitment and not allowing anything to distract you.

WORDS OF WISDOM:

- Write down some of the wise men/women that have shaped your life and why?

"Learn from a wise man and enjoy the journey!"

Read: 2 Corinthians 4:1–12

YOUR THOUGHTS:

YOU CAN MAKE IT

God spoke a very powerful Word to my church one Sunday. We were told that no matter what we face, we will manage because of the spirit of endurance. Endurance is the ability to face anything and everything by maintaining a high level of commitment and excellence. God, through Jesus Christ, empowers and energizes us to go through trials. He empowers us through our convictions and guides us by our sense of call. God allows us to face a myriad of conditions and still come out victorious; in Him, we have all we need to face all we must face.

WORDS OF WISDOM:

- Pay close attention to how people respond to you and how you feel at the end of the day.
- Journal your observations.

"I encourage you to adjust your passion for God and your love and loyalty to Jesus Christ; nothing will discourage you. In this season, willingly endure, trust God for all things, and walk in the power of faith. Believe the best is yet to come. Speak it, live it, and walk it. For God is so faithful that He will ensure your victory despite your challenges."

Read: Romans 5:1–12

YOUR THOUGHTS:

SECOND CHANCES

One Sunday, I was honored to be part of the installation services of an awesome preacher and a rather sizeable congregation. While witnessing this event, I could not help but feel a strong sense of appreciation. My appreciation rested in watching God do what God does best, which is give second chances. I saw a congregation being given a second chance, and at the same time, I saw my own second chance. I saw God open new doors and trust me with greater responsibility. In that moment, I knew God was saying some things to me, and I could not help but worship. My worship was such an inadequate response to His abundant grace and overwhelming mercy.

Look at God, loving us though we are flawed. Look at God, trusting us though we let him down and operate so selfishly. Look at God, opening doors though we mismanage the first open door. Look at God, sending his Son to redeem us though we do not deserve it.

WORDS OF WISDOM:

- Think about your most recent experience when God gave you a second chance.
- List what you are doing to live fully and honor Him in that second chance.

"Let's go after our second chances. It is only in Jesus Christ. Enjoy your day!"

Read: Mark 8:22–26

YOUR THOUGHTS:

THINK YOUR BEST TODAY

We all want to be our best. In order to make this happen, we must think our best. "You are what you think", simply put. What you put in is what will come out.

Norman Vincent Peale, the author of *The Power of Positive Thinking*, says, "You can think yourself to success, or you can think yourself to failure. You can think yourself to victory over your problems, or you can think yourself to defeat by them." The power of your thoughts greatly influences your behavior. If you choose to think victoriously, you will be utterly amazed at the outcome of your life. Thinking your best today involves a few steps:

1. Starting your day out with a PMA (Positive Mental Attitude).
2. Stopping all negative conversation and all negative thoughts.
3. Surrounding yourself with people who think positive.

It is so important that we understand the power of what we believe and what we allow ourselves to think about each day. Your thinking is reflected in your decisions, in your conduct, and in the relationships you form.

WORDS OF WISDOM:

- Guard your mind, and protect your intellectual space.
- Know that your best today is connected to what you are thinking right now!

"Have an awesome thinking day."

Read: Romans 1:18–32; Philippians 4:6–8

YOUR THOUGHTS:

BE YOUR BEST TODAY

God has created you to live a full and healthy life. Within this full and healthy life are opportunities that will propel and promote you to new and exciting places. Each opportunity causes you to grow and expand as a person. God, who has a plan for us, desires one thing and that is for us to be the best we can be.

Being the best we can be means that, with consistency, we give God our absolute all. We strive each day to live above the negative and the nasty and focus on our relationship with Jesus Christ. We yield ourselves over to the Holy Spirit, fulfilling the mandate of Jesus Christ to obey His Word and follow His teachings. Being our best is about living a life that pleases God.

WORDS OF WIDSOM:

- Be your best! Work at life, and work at satisfying God's heart. Give your all and watch God, through your life, do the most amazing things.

"Today, be the best you can be!"

Read: Colossians 3:17

YOUR THOUGHTS:

ARE YOU FAITHFUL?

One of the great themes in Christian faith is that of faithfulness. Many of us feel the pressure to be perfect every day. In fact, we go out of our ways to win the approval of others and to validate ourselves as Christians. Yet God is far more patient and far more willing to walk with us through the process. The partnering of the Holy Spirit with us is a clear sign that God does not desire us to go it alone.

Faithfulness is the best you can do today. Waking up, spending time with God, and then living out the word of His Son Jesus Christ is truly your best. Instead of trying to out-perform others, try just being faithful to God today. Love Him, live for Him, and choose to touch others because of Him. Jesus Christ has shown us that faithfulness is honorable and pleasing to God.

WORDS OF WISDOM:

To maintain faithful, I encourage you to:
- Develop a morning routine that includes prayer & scriptural reflection.
- Connect to a community of believers who can impact you in positive ways.
- Cultivate a spirit of gratitude by "seeing" God as your source for all things!

"Today, be faithful. God will be pleased."

Read: 2 Timothy 4:1–8

YOUR THOUGHTS:

GET UP, GET UP, GET UP!

Life throws all of us curve balls; however, that is not an excuse for believers to give up and throw in the towel. So to put it simply, I am calling you to *get up* and not give up. You have a calling on your life and giving up is not an option. There is no one that can fill your position in life but you.

WORDS OF WISDOM:

- Spend time speaking life to yourself. Refuse to embrace defeat though you are facing it.
- Look for the subtle moments when God reminds you of your destiny. Refuse to ignore who you are in God.
- Go forth in confidence. Refuse to be stagnant, but choose to be excellent, even when you are hurting.

"Know that God has you. Fully embrace God's open door. Get up and be all God has created you to be."

Read: Jeremiah 33:3

YOUR THOUGHTS:

BE GENEROUS

I have learned that one of the most endearing qualities that reflects the nature of God is generosity. Generosity is about giving; it is about opening your hands and allowing some of what you possess to go freely and be a blessing to others. Pure and authentic generosity not only speaks of the heart of God, but it also causes God to extend favor to you. It is an incredible trait. When you make generosity a lifestyle, it partners with everything you desire.

I have learned from my mother the importance of generosity. I have experienced the positive results of God's generosity; over and over, He has abundantly provided for me. Recently, I was reminded that it is because of His generosity that all my needs are met. It was in that moment of revelation that I became even more grateful for my mother and her teachings of generosity.

Generosity is truly your friend. Trust it, and walk with me as I continue to live out this awesome trait of God.

WORDS OF WISDOM:

- Find a new cause that you believe in.
- Make a commitment of generosity to it through donation of time or resources.

"I encourage you to become generous. Give it away, and watch God return it abundantly to you."

Read: Proverbs 11:25, 16:20; John 3:16

YOUR THOUGHTS:

NO LIMITS ON MY MIND

Recently while in a rather intense season of reflection, I began to ruminate about some of my personal limits. It dawned on me that most of those limits are created and nurtured in my mind. The truth is that I am what I think I am, and I can only do what I believe. In that moment, the Holy Spirit began to combat my limits with Philippians 4:13. It was refreshing to hear again the Holy Spirit remind me of the immeasurable authority I walk in as a believer in Jesus Christ. It also reminded me of the importance my mind and my thoughts have in influencing the next phase of my life.

It is said that your perception is your reality. As we approach each new season or situation in our lives, it is our personal interpretations of each circumstance that determine our behavioral responses. We deal with new situations from the present maturity levels of our mindsets. When our minds are cluttered, our limits are many and authoritative. However, when our minds are free of clutter and focused on the positives (Philippians 4:8), we live victoriously free from unnecessary limits.

God, in turn, only allows us to experience that which is consistent with His desire for us. We can seek Him if we desire, or we can remain spiritually aloof. This will affect our ability to respond accordingly and see the positive lessons and messages in any season. It is our intimacy with God that gives us the capacity to see the best in all things and rise above the limits caused in our minds.

WORDS OF WISDOM:

- Through reflection, identify and write what you consider as your limits.
- Intensify your reading of the Word of God about faith and trust in God.

"Look honestly and openly at your limits, and refuse to be controlled by them."

Read: Philippians 4:10–13

YOUR THOUGHTS:

TRUST GOD

As we begin to trust God more, God becomes more valuable in our lives. Trusting God removes the guesswork created by our need to know and understand all things. It accomplishes this through trust as we let go of our need to control. Through our trust and confidence in God, we say confidently, "God I know you control all things, so I let go, and I follow you today."

Trusting God is paramount to a better life because (1) it lessens the stress that results from not knowing what God has next for us; (2) it causes us to seek Him in all things; and (3) it causes us to value God more.

WORDS OF WISDOM:

- Know God has so much more for you;
- Trusting God causes you to have a better journey.

"Work at trusting God, and watch him do amazing things with and through you."

Read: Proverbs 3:5–10

YOUR THOUGHTS:

NEW DOORS ARE OPENING

I woke up one morning with a new revelation. It was so refreshing to hear God declare that for all who will obey Him, new doors are opening. New doors are fresh opportunities that God orchestrates. He creates these opportunities to push us into a radical faith operation mode. New doors are those moments in which God provides, which propels us into a season of major moments and incredible revelations.

WORDS OF WISDOM:

- Properly align yourself in relationships by allowing God to place persons in your life who are connected to Him in a unique way.
- Spend quality time studying and reflecting on the Word of God. The Word is always important in these seasons.
- Obey God and refuse to be intimidated by what you do not understand. Just go with God.
- Think bigger than your situation. Allow faith to push you into exciting places with God.

"Hear God and walk through the new door."

Read: Romans 12:1–2

YOUR THOUGHTS:

MANAGE THE FAMILIAR

I was preparing to preach in Washington, DC, for Pastor Willie Wilson of the Union Temple Baptist Church when a powerful thought hit me. It was my fifth year doing their New Year Revival. Each year, I challenged myself to present the message, as fresh as possible, despite the sense of familiarity I had with the event. In my time of morning reflection, it dawned on me that the blessing of being familiar is that it gives us the wonderful opportunity to showcase our growth.

Familiarity can be either an ally or an enemy of growth. If God's will is for you to remain in a particular place, you must learn how to stay fresh, even if you have mastered the terrain. Familiarity will not harm or hurt you if there is a passion for personal growth and development.

Relationships stay fresh after years because the partners within the relationship strive to stay open to change and available to improving themselves. Employment at a company can be fulfilling after several years because one continues to evolve, growing with the technology and the innovation of the day. Participation in a church can be growth-oriented when one focuses on his or her personal relationship with Jesus Christ, and awakens to the possibilities of what God is doing and saying each day.

WORDS OF WISDOM:
- Spend time reading books and articles that offer a different perspective than what you currently believe.
- In your prayer time, allow God to challenge you with deeper insight into life. Be open to exploring new places.
- Look for moments in the familiar that speak of growth and celebrate.

"Today, though some of you exist in the familiar, stay open. Familiar may be your greater revelation. God, grant us grace in moments of growth. Guide us in finding those moments and celebrating our new opportunities!"

Read: Genesis 1 (as a reminder that you serve the God who creates)

YOUR THOUGHTS:

AND HOW WILL YOU BE REMEMBERED

One day I read an article about Dr. Martin Luther King Jr. It focused on his life, sermons, speeches, leadership, and his courage. Each year on his birthday, we celebrate him. Throughout the year, we are also reminded of his tremendous gifts to each of us. He was a man of great strength.

Yet as we celebrate Dr. King for his amazing journey, I ask you, how will you be remembered? How will your family, friends, and acquaintances remember you? What will be the testimony of those who knew you well?

These are questions I want you to seriously think about. Your life should be of such quality that others want to model themselves after you. When your life ends, you will then be remembered and celebrated. It is easy to say, but how is this accomplished?

WORDS OF WISDOM:

- Always treat others with respect.
- Discover your gift, and perform at your highest level.
- Live your life with passion.
- Love God through your words and your actions.

"Take advantage of the awesome opportunity God has granted you, and live each day with a sense of divine calling. Be blessed."

Read: 2 Timothy 2:1–6

YOUR THOUGHTS:

ENJOY LIFE

The Lord spoke deeply to me one morning. He said, "Son, enjoy life." It was a powerful yet simple moment. God said to me, "Enjoy life." The challenge many of us have is that we allow life to overwhelm us, and we lose our passion. It was in that moment that I saw the simple yet complex nature in the Word of the Lord. I believe God desires us to be complete and whole. We desire more, however, and we continuously choose to struggle and focus on the negative. We let bad days become bad weeks. Bad weeks become bad months. Bad months become a bad year ... and on and on, which ultimately leads to a bad life.

Life is for the living, and on this journey, I challenge you to live and enjoy life.

WORDS OF WISDOM:

Wake up and go about your day with:
- The best attitude you can muster.
- Words that are exciting and encouraging.
- A deepened prayer-life that grounds you.
- A commitment to praise and give God thanks all day.

"Trust God with all you have. Put the biggest smile on your face and enjoy your life!"

Read: Psalm 34

YOUR THOUGHTS:

ARE YOU ON-COURSE?

Are you on-course? This question simply means, are you focused on the goals, projects, and commitments you have made for your life? Are you engaging in activities to accomplish your goals? Are you staying passionate? It is so important that you understand that each day God grants, He allows us to complete something. Completion is vital. When one completes something, it creates a rare sense of peace and joy. With completion comes a sense of satisfaction, and even though challenges may arise, you meet them with confidence as you follow through on your path.

It is important that you ask yourself these questions:

1. Am I staying focused on my goals?
2. Am I manifesting the traits I stated I wanted to work on?
3. Am I working the processes needed to complete what I desire?

WORDS OF WISDOM:

- Post your goals in a prominent place so you "encounter" them every day.
- Do daily, weekly, and monthly reviews to stay focused on accomplishing your goals.
- Stay open to change in your process of evaluation; take a new path if your dreams are not realized.

"Decide that you will finish and go forth with confidence that God, in you, will do greater things. Stay on course. Finish what you start!"

Read: Luke 13:6–9; John 6:1–15

YOUR THOUGHTS:

DON'T JOURNEY ALONE

Take five minutes and list your closest friends; identity why you are so connected to each other and what you need and require of them.

Today, I encourage you to choose not to journey alone. Understand that walking with Jesus Christ does not require you to walk alone. Walking with Him is about relationships with others who love Him as well. Jesus Christ, our Lord, did not walk alone. In fact, He chose twelve men to walk with Him. In His darkest moment, Jesus Christ allowed others to share His space.

WORDS OF WISDOM:

- Look at your circle.
- Ask God to grant you the joy of journeying with others who love Him and who love you unconditionally.

"God has not created us to walk alone. The journey is challenging enough. Through others, God give us a support to manage the journey."

Read: 2 Corinthians 5:17–20

YOUR THOUGHTS:

THIRTEEN YEARS AND STILL GOING STRONG

Amazing! Thirteen years! In 1996, my family and I arrived in Jacksonville, Florida, with my daughter, Alexis, who was three at that time. I was also a few pounds lighter. My beautiful wife still looks exactly as wonderful as she did thirteen years ago. I must admit, our journey together has been awesome. I want to offer you some lessons I've learned over these past thirteen years, lessons that will aid you in your desire to have healthy growth.

WORDS OF WISDOM:

- Identify a set of core values and commit to them.
- Understand that relationships are vital to your growth and your success.
- Admit mistakes, learn from them, and move on.
- Look at life as a marathon, not a sprint.
- Develop the spirit of patience, and trust the process God ordains for you.
- Allow people that are "smarter" than you in a particular area to do what they do. Release the need to be the smartest person in the room.
- Balance the desire for success with a passion for personal development.
- Keep growing, and see growth as a statement of who God is in you.
- Learn to get away; see it as a time to get refreshed for the next assignment in your life.

"As one of my favorite older members would say, "Every day is a good day!"

Read: Psalm 32:8; Philippians 3:12–14

YOUR THOUGHTS:

FOR MY FUTURE

Pastor Jesse Curney of New Mercies Christian Church in Lilburn, Georgia, preached at my church one Sunday. The experience was life changing. His sermon dealt with the importance of guarding your decisions when you are in difficult times. In essence, no matter how bad it seems, a famine is not the time to make a permanent decision.

It is easy to allow your decision-making process to be affected by a moment of extreme discomfort. In many cases, that is what we do. Things get tough, and our natural instinct is to seek action to ease the pain. We step into relationships not ordained, or we take on spirits and ideas for the immediate relief of suffering. In the end, these impulsive decisions bring us into a place of disobedience.

Make Godly decisions to guard your future, even when you find it challenging. Understand that God will be faithful. He will honor you in time. God shows Himself as a God of His word by blessing you.

WORDS OF WISDOM:

- Increase your prayer time when you feel overwhelmed.
- Only trust those whom you totally trust spiritually to advise you. This is not the season to trust people whose relationship with Jesus Christ is questionable.
- Discipline your emotions. Do not allow yourself to be driven to respond based solely on what you feel.
- If necessary, disconnect from the physical space by taking a day to drive or a few moments to go sit and quiet yourself.
- Allow your friends to pray for you and with you. Connect to everyone in the spirit. Let them become your intercessors. The more people that are praying for you, the better you will be.

"Make decisions for the long term. Fight against impulsiveness, and remember, this is for the future."

Read: 2 Kings 6:24, 7:2

YOUR THOUGHTS:

IT'S TRASH DAY

Every Monday is trash day in my neighborhood. We go through the house and gather what we no longer need or use. Once the trash is gathered and bagged, we take it out of the house and place it on the curb for pick-up. We do this to avoid clutter and to remove odors. Everyone in the neighborhood participates in trash day. It is an important day.

Sunday is the believer's trash day. It is the day we come to the house of God to hear the Word of God. This is the day we decide enough is enough; we need to get rid of some "trash." Trash equates to sin and unhealthy behavior. Trash is thoughts that hinder our growth and disrupt our spiritual development.

God calls us to get rid of trash. Decide that this Sunday will be trash day. Open yourself to God, allow God to show you how to gather any "trash" in your life, and through confession, dispose of it.

WORDS OF WISDOM:

- Seek Him for fresh revelation.
- Gather the trash, gather the sin, gather the negative behavior, gather the negative patterns and cycles, gather the negative ways of thinking, and bring them to Jesus Christ for His disposal.
- God loves you and wants the best for you. See you in the Temple. Sunday is coming. Time to take out the trash!

"Uncluttering your life is a requirement to walking in the abundance that God has ordained you for."

Read: Hebrews 12:1–4

YOUR THOUGHTS:

SELF-LOVE

Where does healthy love begin? Of course it begins through God. Any meaningful expression of love must find its genesis in the source of love. However, after God, love must transition from God to us. This means it is healthy to love yourself. In fact, Jesus declared in Matthew 22:39 that neighborly love found its genesis in self-love. Self-love is vital to any form of love. To love yourself means that you value, in an appropriate manner, what God created you to be. As a result, you do not take anyone's purpose or place in life lightly. Out of self-love flows healthy, neighborly love. When I start with me, I can secure that area in my life and reach out to others who are ordained to experience the love of God in me.

WORDS OF WISDOM:

Self-love is possible when:
- You celebrate daily the fact that God loves you.
- You are able to forgive yourself and not allow mistakes to obstruct your growth.
- You see others as a welcome addition to your life.
- You learn to enjoy being alone, and you see those times not as lonely but as aloneness.

"Embrace self-love, not arrogantly but as a necessary piece to the puzzle of healthy humanity. Know that God is secure. He can handle it. Enjoy you, and don't be afraid of what loving yourself means."

Read: Matthew 22:24–40

YOUR THOUGHTS:

FINALLY

I have successfully, with the help of a number of very important people, completed my doctorate of ministry degree. It is starting to sink in that this five-year journey is *finally* complete. As is my tendency, I have spent some time thinking through the process and assessing lessons I've gleaned along the way. It is clear to me that the entire process was as much a teacher and tutor as it was the pursuit of an advanced degree. I am a better person for the process, and without it, I would be less than the man God is calling me to be.

WORDS OF WISDOM:

- The process God ordains for you will be mixed with your choices and, at times, your delays.
- Even with that, God honors you by patiently creating people and resources you need for completion.

"Your finally is on the way."

Read: Jeremiah 29:7–11

YOUR THOUGHTS:

STAY THE COURSE

Every person who is called to do anything great for God will face distractions. The distractions come in the form of relationships, habits, lifestyle practices, challenging situations, or just an intense season of pain and disappointment. Whatever the form of your distraction, you must be willing to face it with courage and decide that nothing will keep you from the will of God.

In watching my parents, I have discovered that if you allow things to get in the way of your day, you will never complete anything. If you allow failure and disappointment to overtake you, you will always feel unbalanced and uneasy in the place of God's will. Your focus should be to stay the course of God's will and to move forward with what God has for you.

WORDS OF WISDOM:

Staying the course requires you to:
- Admit your mistakes.
- Embrace the lessons you've learned.
- Make the necessary adjustments.
- Reaffirm the purpose of your life.
- Limit the negative voices around you.
- Go after God like never before.

"Distractions come. Do not allow them to draw you away from the calling God has placed on your life. Enjoy your journey. It's always good. It's all God."

Read: Psalm 34

YOUR THOUGHTS:

SHAKE IT UP

Are you tired of the direction your life has taken? Do you feel that God has more for you? Do you see your relationships as draining and unfulfilling?

Shake it up! Go deeply into a season of prayer, and ask the Lord to direct your steps to where He desires you to be and what He desires you to do. Understand that if you are living in a place (emotionally and relationally) where you feel empty and ineffective, it may be time to *shake it up!* God has not created you to walk in this place. There are times we must courageously face our life, decide to follow our instincts, and do something about our dissatisfaction.

Shaking it up begins with honestly confronting the present and, if necessary, acknowledging the issues from the past that continue to affect us now. It is about dealing with life from the perspective of the person God desires you to be and not from the perspective of who you presently are. The outcome of the confrontation is clarity. Clarity, in turn, allows you to urgently set your mind on the course that God has ordained for you. *Shake it up!*

WORDS OF WISDOM:
- Sensitize your ear. Let God clearly speak to you at any time regarding where He desires you to go. This includes your conversations, as well as, the sermons and teachings you experience.
- Read the thoughts of successful people, and allow them to mentor and motivate you.
- Operate in urgency! Make the decisions *now*, based on the information you have from God *now* about you *now*.

"Shake it up!"

Read: Mark 8:22–26; Luke 9:51

YOUR THOUGHTS:

SMELL THE ROSES

Life can easily get away from you. Be careful or the days will slip by with you looking back on many missed moments. Moments are designed by God to encourage you and to keep you energized for the remainder of the journey. In these moments, you must learn to stop and smell the roses. This means allowing yourself to breathe and experience the beauty of life. God has created an amazing world and you must decide to enjoy it. This involves seeing the awesome moments in every day and soaking them up as flowers in the sun!

What does this mean? It means when God gives you a great moment, savor it. Live in the moment.

WORDS OF WISDOM:

- Smell the roses.
- Today there might be areas that God is at work on in your life. Now is your time to sit back and smell the roses.
- Celebrate your growth and your progress.
- Learning to enjoy these moments will help you appreciate your many tomorrows.

"Celebrate where God has you and what God is doing with you."

Read: Psalm: 34:1–10

YOUR THOUGHTS:

SEE THE POSSIBILITES

"I thank God for who I am. Because of you I can stand. I thank you God for being a much better man." These words come from a song I experienced in worship one Sunday. As I mulled over these simple words, it dawned on me that the strength of these words rests in the fact that God gives us permission to celebrate the people we are. Understand that this is neither in arrogance nor privilege on our parts; rather we are celebrating who we are with a deep reverence for God's lovingly creative work.

Many people spend their lives looking for the future to be better and for them to be better. At some point, everyone is guilty of spending days projecting on tomorrow. The danger in this process is forgetting to fully embrace today and who you are in the moment.

The person you are right now is a good thing. It says that God's work in your life has truly produced someone that can be trusted with the stewardship of a new day. Self-love is truly a gift from God that we all must properly appreciate. We must learn to ascribe healthy value to ourselves in light of God's love and mercy.

WORDS OF WISDOM:

The person who walks in healthy, holy self-love will:
- Handle rejection better.
- Forgive easier.
- Never allow successes to create arrogance.
- Always live in the spirit of worship.

"Today I grant you permission to love who you are and where you are. Be open to growing; however, stop occasionally to celebrate the person God's grace has produced."

Read: Matthew 22:34–40

YOUR THOUGHTS:

CLEAN IT UP

I was in my office at the church recently, frantically looking for something that I desperately needed. Out of frustration, I ended my search and began to recreate the document. After a minute or two, it dawned on me that it might be buried under the clutter, so I started cleaning up my office. Sure enough, there it was, buried under other piles of junk.

This morning as I pulled myself out of bed, I thought of that day. I thought about how complicated our lives become as a result of decisions we make and issues we refuse to address ... like the piles of junk on my desk.

The challenge is to maintain as simple a life as possible. Managing each day and experience is important to avoid becoming overwhelmed and drained. Many of us allow our private space to become cluttered and disorderly. We invite people in who demand more than is healthy, and we take on habits that pull us from our God-center. In the end, every day is filled with unnecessary drama, and our ability to please God is greatly diminished! We find it difficult to focus on our relationships with Jesus Christ because there are so many *thoughts* and *things* going on. We are overwhelmed with projects God never intended us to do. Busy, busy, busy, the mind rarely has any downtime—time to just relax and hear the voice of God. It is full of *clutter* and it needs to be *cleaned up!*

Is this you? Did I just describe your life? Well if I did, my advice is simply, *clean it up!*

WORDS OF WISDOM:

- Honestly discern what God's will is for your life. This will determine what you clean out!
- Openly and honestly address the issues that are cluttering your life. Have the courage to deal with them and the desire to clean up your life.
- Consistently spend time in prayer and devotion, and keep the voice of God before you. Remember that your time with

God will positively affect your ability to stay on the cutting edge of God's will.

- Journal your thoughts daily, and allow them to shape your understanding of life and purpose.
- Stay in a place of growth by building a circle of healthy friends who can speak into your life.

"My friends, no more excuses. Clean it up!"

Read: Hebrews 12:1–2

YOUR THOUGHTS:

SIT, LISTEN, LEARN, AND APPLY

A few years ago, a great couple in my church gave me a gift of free golf lessons. Now mind you, I am not much of a golfer. I play well enough to be frustrated at a bad shot, so the lessons were much appreciated. Unfortunately, I soon learned that because I had formed so many bad habits, it was difficult for me to change. In the end, the lessons—though they provided a great getaway—never translated into my becoming a better golfer; those bad habits just kept getting in the way. I was able to sit at the feet of a golf pro, but I couldn't move past myself to heed his advice. Even today, I still do certain things on the golf course that work against my score.

The average believer performs in life just how I perform on the golf course. Habits that are not good for us are cemented through our refusal to follow the advice of our teachers/mentors. We continue to live life beneath our potentials due to our inability to move beyond our bad habits. Many of us would be much farther along if we followed the process of today's devotional: *sit, listen, learn, and apply.*

The "average" believer does not have a recognized mentor—someone empowered to call them into accountability. This aspect of your Christian life is important because healthy growth flows from healthy relationships. The presence of someone who can and will commit to your personal development is priceless. In certain seasons, this person is more valuable than anything; he or she equips you to navigate potential landmines while pointing you in a direction of destiny and purpose. Coupled with this, he or she challenges you to grow and, when necessary, corrects you. This is an essential factor in your readiness to go where God wants to take you. Healthy relationships are a must.

WORDS OF WISDOM:

- Assess your relationships today, and seek God's direction.

"My life consists of several important people who loves God enough to love me, while participating in my growth process."

Read: 2 Kings 2

YOUR THOUGHTS:

FOCUS ON THE EXPERIENCE

I am not an *American Idol* fan. In fact, I never watch the show. Yet recently, I was watching a television show, and two of the finalists were being interviewed. During the course of the interview, the second place finisher made an awesome statement. The interviewer pushed him on whether he was disappointed in his second place finish. Looking intently in the interviewer eyes, the second place winner responded (I am paraphrasing here), "Winning was not my goal. Taking advantage of the opportunity and doing my best in the moment was."

My spirit leaped! That is exactly what God wants to hear from you each and every day! The fact is that winning is not about being better than the other person; it is about maximizing the moment God gives you. It dawned on me that the door is only open a moment, and if you are not careful, the moment will pass. So many are then left and miss the moment. Yes, the door passed and even worse, it closed.

Pray: "Lord, make me sensitive to your voice so I will never miss an opportunity to do my best."

WORDS OF WISDOM:

- God is opening new doors, and I encourage each of you to develop an ear for His voice in order to move in concert with Him.
- Let's take the American Idol finalist's advice and not focus on winning. Focus on the experience. What great advice!

"Opportunities only matter when you see the God in them. In that moment, you embrace the door and confidently walk through it."

Read: Jeremiah 29:4–14

YOUR THOUGHTS:

AND THIS TOO SHALL PASS

For every person that walks with Jesus Christ, there is a season that appears just too incredibly unbearable. The pain, sacrifice, and suffering we experience causes numbness; this leaves us groping for a way out or temporary relief from the pain. Praying and reading becomes work. We wonder where God is in the midst of our failing. Often accompanied by relationship pain, physical pain, or emotional pain, this season drains us and weakens our faith. In an attempt to resolve our conflict, we look anywhere for advice.

The key to this season is not a magical or mystical revelation that answers all the questions. Success requires a tenacity to fight through. It requires you to wake up every morning and to continue on the path of wellness by doing those normal things you did in seasons when things were well. It is about reading when you get nothing out of it. It is about praying when you are distracted. It is about writing when you feel empty. It is about serving when it seems laborious and boring. It is about fighting through with a tenacity that is birthed in us through our worship lives. Our time spent with God develops this tenacity; the ongoing nurturance of your relationship with God will see you through these times even when you see no immediate benefit.

I write this because there may be some of you who deeply love God; however, you are currently in a really dry place. Believe me, I have been there. I have asked, "Where are you God, and why is this happening to me?" My answer was focused on staying on my positive course—doing whatever God had called me to do and continuing to do it consistently. This doesn't end the season, but know that God is producing something awesome.

WORDS OF WISDOM:

- Fight through this season and stay faithful to God. Just stay faithful!
- Believe that God is faithful to you and that the pain will produce His glory.

As my mother would say, "And this too shall pass."

Read: Psalm 62

153

YOUR THOUGHTS:

CELEBRATE AS YOU GO

When I spoke at the graduation exercises for Highland Middle School here in Jacksonville, one of my dear friends and I started talking. He jokingly commented on the many graduation experiences children have today.

I thought about it and decided that more graduations are a good thing. Every time a child is allowed to celebrate, it deepens their sense of accomplishment and encourages them to continue on the path toward their higher goals. The wise parent, in turn, uses these accomplishments to nurture healthy self-esteem in his or her child.

While this concept is important for the child, it is also important for you as an adult believer. It is important that you learn to celebrate the milestones of your journey with Jesus Christ. Celebrating as you go encourages a focus on the next milestone. It fuels the fire in you to go after what God has designed for you. It empowers you to face your challenges and trials because you know they are temporary. It makes every experience a tutor, teaching and instructing you for the next stage. In the end, it keeps joy alive within your life as the spirit of praise drips from your lips constantly.

WORDS OF WISDOM:

- I encourage you to celebrate as you go.
- Stop, and as David did, dance before the Lord as a way of celebrating how far God has brought you and how close you are to the ultimate goal of your journey.
- Find a reason to dance, and choose to celebrate as you go!

"Stop and enjoy every accomplishment, no matter how small. They all assist in making you GREAT!"

Read: 2 Samuel 6; Psalm 34

YOUR THOUGHTS:

DEVELOP A FIVE-STAR LIFE

My church has a special time that has become affectionately known as daddy/daughter time. The goal is to recapitulate the points from a Mother's Day sermon I preached, titled *My Fair Lady*. I chose to review this sermon in a smaller teaching setting because, although the sermonic moment is powerful, there is something special about sharing lessons from the sermon in small groups.

During the course of our small group time together, the Spirit led me to discuss with them the value of names and reputations. The key to a name, I shared, is paying the price for a life of excellence. In essence, it is fine that one talks of excellence, but at some point, you must perform at a level of excellence. This means developing a life of excellence, or as I call it, a five-star life.

We are all familiar with a five-star hotel. It earns its five-star rating because it strives to exceed expectations of its guests. Its goal is to provide excellent service. A five-star life is very similar to that of a five-star hotel. It describes a life of intentional excellence, where one strives to perform at the highest level while being governed by standards that are reflections of God and His creative intent for humanity. A five-star life is about exceeding expectations and giving your best. God has called us to live at a high level and to achieve His will in the earth. His will is something that deserves and demands excellence.

WORDS OF WISDOM:

- The genius of your life is that you will be hungry for excellence along with a desire to pay the price for it.
- The perfect example of this is Jesus Christ, whose sacrifice so exceeded expectations that, even today, we are still living in His gift and being transformed by His love.
- Choose to live a five-star life. God will honor you for the effort!

"Be your best and God will trust you with the best!"

Read: 1 Kings 10; Romans 8:12–17

YOUR THOUGHTS:

WHAT IS YOUR ADDICTION?

I woke up one morning to my normal routine. I reached to turn on my cell phone—a small part of my daily ritual. The night before, I had experienced a few problems with the connection; however, with charging, I figured the problem would be corrected. But to my surprise, that morning my phone, which was considered one of the best on the market, refused to work. Thirty minutes later, I gave up and turned to my television system only to discover that it, too, had developed amnesia. No sound came through the surround system, and the screen was blank.

I became anxious. I didn't know what to do! No phone, no television ... I was frustrated as I looked around at everything not working. My cell phone was dead, and the television was not working. As I sat frustrated it hit me: *I was addicted.* My day was laced with extras that had become essentials. My morning required a cell phone for texting and a television for noise. Instead of enjoying the quiet of the morning, I was quietly frustrated about the inoperable state of the gadgets in my life.

How many of you are like me, too dependent on things to assist you in your transition in the morning? I discovered that I needed the distractions. I needed the noise of television and the access to others in the morning. Today I admit it! I am addicted to my gadgets.

I am not the only one who wakes up in the morning and turns on noise. I am not the only one who wakes up and immediately accesses the outside world. This morning I decided to revamp my morning. I made a decision to spend the first part of the morning in quiet, to reflect more while writing and reading on God and the life He has created for me. Know that God desires our time and attention too! At the end of the day, God is truly the source of all the good in our lives.

WORDS OF WISDOM:

- Learn to enjoy the quiet;
- Intentionally disconnect from the outside world by shutting down its conduits;

- See your time as your time; have the courage to manage it for your personal growth;
- Remove the complex realities of today and find peace in the simpler things.

"Loving God must become our ultimate passion. Place God first and all things will work out."

Read: Matthew 6:25–33

YOUR THOUGHTS:

FIND YOUR PLACE IN THE WORLD

I love being a pastor. It allows me to relate to the members of Saint Paul. I also love the opportunity to share the transforming message of Jesus Christ. Sharing His message is the most exhilarating thing in my life.

It is incredible to wake up in the morning and love what you do. Nothing replaces or supplants the desire to love what you do. Finding your place in the world with no restraints, equipping and preparing yourself to do your best at the highest level in what you love is an amazing feeling.

God has granted you the grace to live with destiny and purpose. This destiny and purpose provides the energy to face both the good and bad days. No matter what you face, you persevere. Your destiny and purpose holds you tightly to God and empowers you to live free.

Seek God for what you are created, called, and gifted to do. Finding your place in this vast world is amazing; living it out until you have nothing left is even more amazing. If you are a janitor, be the best janitor you can be; if you are a doctor, be the best doctor you can be; if you are a teacher, be the best teacher you can be; if you are a housewife, be the absolute best at it that you can be. Whatever you are, make sure it is what God has called for you.

WORDS OF WISDOM:

- When you wake up in the morning, do you love what you do?
- If your answer is yes, list ways that you can do it better.
- If you answered no, begin the challenge to search for what gifts God has given to you

"God has created you with the ability to enjoy life and to love what you do. If you are not in that place yet, sincerely ask God to show you the way, and trust the path he sets for you. Enjoy the journey."

Read: John 6:37–38

YOUR THOUGHTS:

WHEN I MOVE, YOU MOVE

My family and I are the proud owners of a beautiful Golden Lab named Angel. Each morning as I write and meditate, Angel is right beside me. The interesting thing is that when I move, Angel not only moves, but she moves as if we are one, never getting too far away from me. When she is in the room with me, she lies quietly next to the chair. When I get up, for any reason, her tendency is to get up and follow me. When I return to the chair, she quietly lies down again. Amazingly, she lies in the same place, relaxed and at peace. As long as I am sitting down in that chair, she is fine right where she lies. She only moves when I move.

Angel teaches us a valuable life lesson about our relationships with God. Sadly, Angel does a better job of relating than most of us do. She is wise enough to trust my presence; however, when it comes to God, many of us are antsy and anxious. In this, we get ahead of God and engage in activities that God does not ordain. We become frustrated and make decisions that are beneath what God desires for us. Yet a dog named Angel teaches us that when we trust and value our owner's presence, we will quietly rest until He moves. This trust in God stems from a healthy worship-life, nurtured through a daily devotional-life and grounded in a deep passion for God.

WORDS OF WISDOM:

- Learn to invoke the presence of God and rest.
- Dwell so consistently in the presence of God that nothing distracts or disrupts your time with Him.
- God will spill over into every facet of your life, and you will find each day strangely calm, even in the midst of challenges and crisis.

"Look for opportunities to just rest in the presence of God. And when God moves, you move!"

Read: Luke 10:38–42

YOUR THOUGHTS:

FACE IT!

It is amazing how farther along you would be if you were willing to face us. Not the "us" that others celebrate or even the "us" you present to others, but the "us" that Jesus died for. To face us, you must be open to correction and, sometimes, rebuke. Correction means you must be willing to accept the intentional calling out of behavior and attitudes that hinder your deeper commitment to Jesus Christ. Often correction is turned into a reason to evaluate the voice of the corrector or is seen as a personal attack. The result is feeling victimized and becoming surrounded with people who guard a fragile ego. A potentially wonderful moment of growth is therefore missed; God then allows experience to become the teacher because he could not employ relationships for the task. Is this you? Do you struggle to hear honesty? Do you become religiously defensive?

Be grateful that God loves you enough to create opportunities for you to face you; these are the opportunities for you to begin the process of fixing areas of your life that interfere with you being who God designed. The mere fact that God speaks so caringly and so clearly is indication that your life has value to Him. Face it so you can fix it. Come to terms with those things that inhibit your full greatness, and trust God for the strength to see the process through. Face it so you can fix it!

WORDS OF WISDOM:

- Make a list of thing of things you need to face.
- Pray and ask God to give you the strength to face those things so you can fix them.

"You can't fix what you will not face."

Read: Hebrews 12:1–11

YOUR THOUGHTS:

ENJOY GOD'S NATURE

Enjoying the soothing sounds of nature one evening, I was overjoyed at how clearly God chose to communicate with me. It wasn't in a Rhema word or in some audible voice; rather it was just the clear sounds of nature. The frogs were croaking, the wind was blowing, and nature was just chattering away. I sat there intrigued, enjoying God's other voice—His nature voice.

Find a place in your world where God can speak to you. Allow Him to use nature as the conduit for His voice. Open up your heart to God, and enjoy the awesome way God says, "I am still here, and I am in charge."

WORDS OF WISDOM:

- Let God do what only God will do.
- Let God love you in the quiet of the night using nature to speak.
- Take time to enjoy God and watch how simple life becomes.

"Decide that this day would conclude with my Father allowing me to sit at His feet and hear Him talk. Enjoy God in all His greatness!"

Read: Psalm 19

YOUR THOUGHTS:

ARE YOU EXCITED YET?

Are you excited about your life? Are you thrilled to wake up every day, feeling the wonderful weight of God's presence? Isn't it exciting to know that God has your future in His hands? If you trust Him, all will work out for your benefit. I sense that there are others who feel God's hands on your life. It is an amazing feeling to know that God has you and that He is working through your issues and flaws to achieve His purpose in your life. Yes, I said your issues and flaws. Know that even when you are not all that you should be, God still uses you to produce His purpose in the earth. Your issues may cause others to doubt you, but God never has any doubt. God allows for your transgressions and yet continues to love you, all the while using you for His purposes. God gives you grace to grow, and if you are open to His grace through worship, He will love you through it all.

As my friend Melanie Clark says, "Fast from negative thinking and confessions today." Love on God, and enjoy the power of now! *Be excited and watch God do the amazing!*

WORDS OF WISDOM:

- Awaken the spirit of excitement in you. Open up to the depth of His love, and find the joy to enjoy this day.
- Find God in this day, and enjoy all that comes with Him.
- God, through Christ, claims and celebrates you. Enjoy today!

"Don't wait till the battle is over. Shout now!"

Read: Psalm 34:1–8

YOUR THOUGHTS:

ACCEPT THE CHALLENGE

Too many Christians live the life of someone else. God has called you to do one thing. Somehow, you are stuck doing something else. You are walking on a path that was not paved for you, dancing in shoes that were not made for you, and kicking in doors that are not supposed to be open to you.

God is challenging you to live the life He has designed just for you. No matter how difficult the challenge is, God has decided that you cannot walk in anything less than His purpose and plan for you. God is clearly declaring, "Accept the challenge!" Nothing will distract you or deter you from the Will of God.

WORDS OF WISDOM:

Accept the challenge and resolve the following:
- Self-esteem issues - believe in who you are in God.
- Relationships - surround yourself with persons who encourage God's Will and purpose.
- Unresolved sin - be willing to deal with this area of your life.
- Unforgiveness - unclutter your heart and be willing to release others.
- Devotional life - Commit to setting aside time to spend with God.

"In the power of God's authority, remove your burdens. Accept the challenge!"

Read: Joshua 1:1–9

YOUR THOUGHTS:

TAKE A PRAISE BREAK

On Monday night, Major League Baseball hosted its annual Home Run Derby. After each contestant took his swing, a young person quickly handed him a towel and a bottle of Gatorade. The Gatorade allowed players to get refreshed for the next round.

When it comes to you, what is your refreshing beverage? What keeps you energized for the next round? The answer is your *praise*. Praise is your refreshment. When you are tired from doing your best at each level, praise empowers you and gets you ready for what's next.

WORDS OF WISDOM:

- Stop what you are doing, and celebrate God in your life. Today is the day to stop and sip from the presence of God's well.

"Celebrate God by taking a praise break!"

Read: 2 Samuel 6

YOUR THOUGHTS:

THIRSTY

While sitting on a plane and listening to one of my favorite artists, Pastor Jason Nelson, I had a reflective moment. As Pastor Nelson sang "Thirsty," I wondered how many of us in the Body of Christ understand what the phrase *thirsty for God* means. The insatiable need for the presence of God supplants everything else. Nothing compares to being with God and spending time with Him. To know and desire God through Jesus Christ is amazing. The mere thought of His love and the inexhaustible nature of His mercy is overwhelming. Many, however, are comfortable with a casual relationship with Jesus Christ.

Thus, it is so important that we, through the intentional use of the spiritual disciplines, develop a thirst for God. Yes, intentional! A willingness to push beyond casual religion into a "place" with God where you desire the Eternal beyond everything! Time to crave God! Stay thirsty!

WORDS OF WISDOM:

- Today, take time and write down why you love and need Jesus Christ.
- Use this as a guide to strengthening your personal worship-life.
- Devote time today to allow God to speak to your heart by declaring how deeply you love Him.

"Today, feel your need for God until you reach the place of no God, no me."

Read: Psalm 68

YOUR THOUGHTS:

GOD WANTS SOME TIME

When was the last time you spent a day with God? I'm not talking about a five-minute prayer moment or a casual conversation while in the car to work with the radio blaring. When is the last time you actually set aside a day or even a couple of hours to spend alone with God?

What separates saints from churchgoers is just this—time. The saint deeply craves the presence of God and intentionally creates time for Him. The saint goes out of the way to spend time with God and refuses to allow any invasion of that space. The saint sees time with God as a time to draw closer to the Father. He or she deeply values the voice of God. The saint wants nothing short of a meaningful, transforming intimacy with God.

A person who lives like this develops a lifelong relationship with God. This kind of time spent with God:

- Clarifies your purpose;
- Clears your mind of clutter;
- Reinforces your values;
- Exposes negative people and places;
- Redirects your focus to your primary relationship, namely with Jesus Christ.

WORDS OF WISDOM:

- Quarterly, set aside a day to go away and be with God.
- Find a place in the world where distractions are minimal and where your focus is intensified.
- In this time and place, listen, pray, read, write, and center yourself. Reconnect with God, and allow Him to reenergize you. Know that your prayer time is vital.

"Focus on God by refocusing on prayer. God has been waiting and now He wants some time!"

Read: Philippians 4:6–9

YOUR THOUGHTS:

DEVELOP A LIFE FILTER

I once had a Rain Soft system installed in my home, which was designed to filter impurities out of tap water. The presentation by the salesman sold me. He first tested our water in its unfiltered state, then bottled water, and finally water filtered through the Rain Soft system. He clearly made his case and showed us that unfiltered water was full of impurities that only the Rain Soft system could get rid of. Once the presentation was over, my wife and I both agreed that for the sake of our quality of life, the Rain Soft system best suited us, and we purchased the system. Why? The evidence of impurities in our present water system was too great to ignore.

Create the same kind of filter using your relationship with Jesus Christ as the filter. Call it a life filter. There is no way you can achieve all God desires for you with impurities in your life. Just like the water, most of the impurities are not obvious or noticeable. They blend into your life so smoothly until everything appears to look normal. Yet, the damage these impurities cause over the long haul is paralyzing and in some cases, permanent.

WORDS OF WISDOM:

- Have the courage to trust your relationship with Jesus Christ.
- Allow the Holy Spirit to reveal your true identity to you. Empower the Holy Spirit to serve as a filter in all areas of your life.

"Allow Jesus Christ to be the Rain Soft system for your life until life's impurities are no longer draining you of all God has for you."

Read: Psalm 51

YOUR THOUGHTS:

I HAD TO DO IT

I attended a friend's funeral in Chesapeake, Virginia. In college, Chris Sessoms and I were the best of friends. In fact, because of Chris, I successfully managed my first year of college at Virginia Tech. Chris was a great guy. His death was a shock, and it brought together hundreds of friends and acquaintances, some from our years at VA Tech.

Over the last few years, he and I had not communicated as much as we had previously; however, to not attend his home-going service would have been a desecration to the relationship we shared. I traveled to pray the Prayer of Consolation. It was one of the most important prayers I had ever prayed. In Chris's honor and to God's glory, I prayed. I had to. That which I had to do, God gave me the strength to do.

In life, there are certain relationships that we must be faithful to no matter what. Real relationships demand sacrifice. Give to these relationships with an attitude of gratitude. Give gladly, for these real relationships are made of true love.

WORDS OF WISDOM:

- Take great pride in your generosity.
- Know that God is pleased.
- Do your bidding, whatever it is, and God will say well done.

"Go forth with gratitude!"

Read: John 14:1–14

YOUR THOUGHTS:

GUEST WRITERS

When God instructed me to write this book, one of the unique qualities of the book was to be a partnership with others who feel an inclination and calling to share their thoughts in written form. It was this strong sense of covenant that motivated me to extend an invitation through an open writers' contest to potential writers. Out of the 100+ submissions, came 25 persons whose thoughts spoke the clearest. With great joy, I present them to you and pray what they share will impact you as much as it has already impacted me.

As one who feels called to aid others in destiny discovery, I found great satisfaction in creating a vehicle by which these amazing men and women can share their gift. You will be blessed as you walk with them through the incredible place of the mind. Listen closely to the voice of God through these 25 men and women of God! Allow them to speak deeply to you, as you seek to know intimately the plan of God for your life. Trust that it is not by accident that you are given moments with the unknown writer, who will one day be not just known but greatly appreciated for their offering of insight and revelation.

Again, thank you for sharing time with us and ENJOY these amazing men and women as they share their thoughts with you. You will truly never be the same again!! Read on...........

YOU'VE GOT HIS WORD

By Dionne Adams
Jacksonville, FL

What great news! What an assurance to know that God is with you and will keep you wherever you go. To know you have *His* protection, His promise and His Word. He will not leave you until He's done all that He's promised you. What great comfort! When God makes a promise, He vows by *His* own name. No other name is higher. His Word will accomplish all that He sends it to do. (Isaiah 55:11)

So, as you walk in the place and the things that only you've heard him say to you, take comfort. He is with you. As you move in faith across the country and away from all that is familiar, resign from your job to start your own business, start an early morning prayer circle on your job for the company and its employees, take heart. He is with you.

As you go fearfully, know He will cover you in the wings of His protection (Psalms 91:4). He will protect you by guiding your decisions and directing your footsteps. He will give you an encouraging word and people to partner with you, and He will open doors of opportunity. *"That's me. I'm here. A light to your path."* He knows the best pathways for your life. He will advise and watch over you (Psalms 32:8); not leaving you until He's done all that He's promised you. *All.* What peace that brings.

So, be encouraged. He's with you! You've got His Word!

Read: Genesis 28:15; Hebrews 6:13–20

PERFECTLY IMPERFECT

By Alexis Alexander
College Park, GA

God, you made all the delicate inner parts of my body and knit me together in my mother's womb. Thank you for making me so wonderfully complex! Your workmanship is marvelous; how well I know it. You watched me as I was being formed in utter seclusion, as I was woven together in the darkness of the womb. You saw me before I was born. Every day of my life was recorded in your book. Every moment was laid out before a single day had passed. How precious are your thoughts about me, O God. They cannot be numbered! (Psalm 139:13–17)

Reader, have you ever looked at yourself in the mirror and picked out everything that was wrong with you? I have, quite a few times, truthfully. The older I get, the more things there are to pick out if I want to. Now I'm not perfect, and I have not yet completely mastered this, but I'm learning to do it less and less.

You see, I have freckles and moles on my face. For the longest time years ago, they secretly bothered me. Many times I would just stare at them as if that would make them disappear. So one day as I stared at the mirror, I heard God tell me clear as day, "I put those there."

So if I believe God (and I do) and that He is sovereign (and He is) and knows what He is doing (He does) and created me and saw fit to put these freckles on my face (He did), then what's the problem? Me and my perception of me.

For the first time I saw them through God's eyes. I no longer have to wish they would disappear. I learned to love them. I now see them as beauty love marks from my Heavenly Father.

So now you ask why I tell you this. Because I don't want you to waste another minute fussing and fighting over things you have no control over. Stop trying to change the very thing that makes you, you! You can't help it if your hair is thin or thick, if your lips are small or big, if your smile is slightly off-centered or straight, if you have one brown eye and one blue eye, or if you have freckles or moles. Look at your imperfections through God's eyes, and realize you are perfectly imperfect. Now that should make you smile.

Enjoy the rest of your day. Smile, knowing that God made you just the way you are and that it's for a reason. Stop fighting it and start loving it!

TEMPTED TO BE OFFENDED? LET IT GO!

By Daree Allen, MS
Suffolk, VA

Every day we have a choice of whether to give in to the temptation or to be offended by something or someone. We can choose whether to react to the offense or to let it go. Someone can betray you or treat you wrongly, or maybe you have hopes that go unfulfilled.

When you decide to stop being offended and let go of a situation, you're no longer anxious about it. You have inner peace. You stop longing for things to be other than they are. You accept life as it comes. Your attitude is patient optimism. You trust that it will all work out for you.

Acknowledge the pain you feel, and then get over it as quickly as possible without reasoning or over-analyzing. The reward in letting go is that your hand is open to receive what's really for you. We grow when we let go. Move on, and know that God has something better for you.

Letting go makes us stronger. It helps us withstand different tests in the future and be examples to people who are watching us, whether it be others that are going through the same thing, people waiting for us to fail, or those that look up to us for advice and direction and as role models.

Questions for Reflection:
1. Read Proverbs 19:11: How should we handle it when someone offends us?
2. Read Psalm 39:7: In whom should we put our hope?
3. Read Jeremiah 29:11: When the plans we hoped for don't work out, what should we
4. remember?
5. Read Romans 8:28: How do we know that things will work for us?

MISSING GOD

By Veronica Bedford
Douglasville, GA

"And without faith it is impossible to please God, for whoever would approach him must believe that he exists and that he rewards those who seek him."
-Hebrews 11:6 NIV

This passage urges those who encounter it to understand the premise of accessing God—faith. Critical to the implementation of faith is that we believe that God exists and rewards those who seek His presence.

While visiting the hair salon one day, I was reading a book for a homework assignment. I came across a passage that caused me pause. Author, Ada Maria Isasi-Diaz, wrote, "True spirituality has to do with living a reflective life, knowing that we are guided by God from within, that we are loved and admired by God. This God who falls in love with us over and over again … waits for us to reciprocate."

As I reflected on the words of the author and the goodness of God in my own life, I became aware of the times we miss (overlook) God. God's presence was so real to me at that moment, but yet everyone else was absorbed in the happenings of the salon. I was greatly moved by the heavenly visitation but grieved by the lack of awareness. I was convicted. How many times have I missed God? Have I been so busy and so overwhelmed that I have overlooked the divine? God falls in love with us over and over again. The proof exists in the new mercies we receive every morning. As people of faith, we must seek God. We must look for God's presence every day in various ways, even in the mundane and chaotic. Otherwise, we will simply continue to miss (overlook) God until we miss (have a longing for) God.

SEEING DETERMINES BEING

By Tavares J. Bussey
New Haven, CT

It's amazing how two people can look at the same thing and come away with two extremely different interpretations. It's quite difficult to look at a thing the way it should be looked at when your perception is based on you and not the thing.

The brain is a finely designed organ. It has the ability to devise thoughts, visions, and ideas. The brain is often referred to as the center of life. Anyone who is brain-dead is incapable of participating in life. Our perceptions of ourselves determine every view and response.

When the twelve spies were sent out to survey the Promised Land of the children of Israel, they came back with a report. All twelve saw the same land, the same people, and the same opportunities, but only two of the spies saw the promise while the rest saw the struggle. When you see yourself beating the odds and being a victor, it's not uncommon to see hard situations as welcomed opportunities to show your belief in hope and victory. The others had perception issues that caused them not to see the promise as Caleb and Joshua saw. They came back with a report that mirrored such small thinking. They saw themselves as "grasshoppers" and couldn't see possessing the Promised Land (Numbers 13).

Daily we must seek to renew our minds and put on the mind of Christ. Our perceptions drive our interpretations; our interpretations drive our responses. If we want to witness and experience promise, then we should disregard pessimistic living that fuels low thinking. If we see things as Christ does, then we'll believe what faith sees and thus speak what faith sees. The promise is before us if we choose to see!

TRUST GOD

By Shaquana Canada
Bridgeport, CT

I sometimes wonder why terrible things have to happen. Is it to make us stronger? I honestly don't know. But what I do know is that everything happens for a reason. There are times when I sit in bed and cry because of how angry I am with God. And then there are days that I wake up so vibrant and pleased with the bond we have, like today for example. I have no clue why things happen or why people leave this world in the prime of their lives, but at the end of the day I know that God has a reason for doing everything. Eventually he will answer all my questions, but for right now, I will trust him and live day by day.

The reason I was so angry was because I lost sight of God and His Word, and my faith became shattered because of my impatience and unwillingness to trust my Father. In order for God to take control of your life, you have to stop intervening when he is in the process of turning your situation around. I used to start trusting God and say, "I surrender all to you," but then I would turn around and do what I wanted to do because God didn't move on my time. In turn, my situation either worsened or stayed the same. I had to learn that God does not move on central or eastern time but on supernatural time. So, I have a little encouragement for anyone going through a trial: trust God. He never fails to amaze me with his love.

COME DOWN THE STAIRS

By Shavon Carter
Bowie, MD

"O my dove, that art in the clefts of the rock, in the secret places of the stairs, let me see thy countenance, let me hear thy voice; for sweet is thy voice, and thy countenance is comely."
-Song of Solomon 2:14 KJV

A couple months ago, I purchased a small dog that I named Teddy Bear. Teddy Bear stands a couple inches high and weighs about twelve pounds. He's a very active dog and enjoys playing and running around. But one thing I've noticed about Teddy Bear is his fear of coming down the stairs.

There's a loft area in my home that's connected to a spiral staircase leading downstairs. Teddy Bear is the kind of puppy that will follow me all around the house, but when I walk down the stairs, I don't hear his footsteps following behind me. When I look up to the loft area, I see his little head peeping through the rails, with sad, puppy-dog eyes. Then he'll walk to the tip of the top stair and lean forward as if he's trying to estimate whether he can make it down that first step. Then he jolts backward and lies down in defeat.

As I watch, I keep encouraging him by saying, "Come down the stairs, Teddy Bear," knowing that if he could overcome his fear, he would be able to roam freely. But the funny thing about it is he has come down the stairs once before while following my friend's dog, which is a little older than him. So I know he has the ability to come down, but he is controlled by fear.

Just like Teddy Bear, many of us have some areas of our lives in which we are afraid to move. You may be on the brink of stepping into something new and different, but because of the fear of making that first step, you stand still. And just as Solomon urges the Shulamite woman to come out of her place of hiding in verse 14, God is watching you and saying, "Come down the stairs." Your stairs of life may be switching careers, starting a business, or writing a book. God has given you everything you need to make it safely, but still you hold back and hesitate. But if only you would take that first step, you will find that the rest of the way is not as bad as you anticipated. Then you can enter into a realm where you will receive blessings you never thought imaginable.

I know it doesn't look like you can make it, and it will require a leap of faith. But remember God's thoughts of you are of peace and not of evil, to give you an expected end. He wouldn't instruct you to come if He didn't plan to keep you as you walk. Trust in Him and be obedient to His call. He has already filled you with the strength and the courage you will need, so just come down the stairs, and walk into your destiny.

OPENED AND CLOSED DOORS

By William Carter
Sacramento, CA

We need to learn to thank the Lord for closed doors just as much as we do for open doors. The reason God closes doors is because He has not prepared anything over there for us.

If he didn't close the wrong doors for us, we would never find our way to the right door. Even when we don't realize it, God directs our paths through the closing and opening of doors. When one door closes, it forces us to change our course. Another door closes, and it forces us to change our course yet again.

Then finally, we find the open door and walk right into our blessing. But instead of praising God for the closed door (which kept us out of trouble), we get upset because we judge by the appearances! And in our own arrogance, or ignorance, we insist that we know what is right.

We have a very present help in the time of need that is always standing guard. Because He walks ahead of us, He can see trouble down the road and *He* sets up road blocks and detours accordingly. But through our lack of wisdom, we try to tear down the roadblocks or push aside the detour signs.

Then the minute we get into trouble, we start crying, "Lord how could this happen to me?"
We have got to realize that the closed door was a blessing. Didn't He say that no good thing will He withhold from them that love Him?

If you get terminated from your job, don't be down; instead, thank God for the new opportunities that will manifest themselves. It might be a better job or an opportunity to go to school. If that man or woman won't return your call, it might not be them; it might be the Lord setting up a roadblock. Just let it go!

For example, a person once had a bank he had been doing business with for many years tell him no for a $10,000 loan. The Lord led him to call another bank. That bank approved a $40,000 loan for him at a lower interest rate than his own bank had advertised.

I'm so grateful for the many times God has closed doors to me, just to open them in the most unexpected places. "The steps of a good man are ordered by the Lord, and He delights in his way" (Psalm 37:23 KJV). The mountaintop is glorious, but it is in the valley that I will grow!

Always remember God gives you enough:
- sorrows to keep you human
- failure to keep you humble
- success to keep you eager
- faith to banish depression
- Determination to make each day a better day than the last

Life must be lived forward but can only be understood backward.

HOW DOES WHOLENESS LOOK?

By Dr. Wendy R. Coleman
Leesburg, GA

You know the great thing about *wholeness* is that it looks different for everything and everyone. Let me explain. A whole banana doesn't look like a whole apple. A whole house doesn't look like a whole boat. A whole cat doesn't look like a whole dog. Get what I'm saying yet? If you do, you might have to put your book down and give God a praise dance right quick! Why? You should have your shouting shoes on because just like nothing existing in nature or made by man looks whole in the way any other thing does, we as people who are pursuing wholeness won't look like anybody else when God brings us to our place of completeness.

Think about it. When Jesus carried out His ministry as retold by the Gospel writers, He encountered a lot of broken, hurting, seeking, searching, pursuing people. Remember the man with the withered hand? He couldn't function fully because there was something non-functioning on his physical body—his hand. The man who was blind has the same type of non-functioning situation going on, but his didn't have to do with his hand; it was his eyes. Then there was the man who had been hanging out by the pool for thirty-eight years; his legs were his non-functioning appendages. But the great thing about Jesus is that *he made all of them whole!*

When Jesus was done working what we refer to as "miracles," making the withered hand strong, the blinded eyes see, and the paralyzed legs walk, each of the men could proclaim the same thing, *"I am whole!"* They had a different story to tell and had gone through a different test, but they all had the same testimony! So rejoice with me, my friend. It doesn't matter what you're going through—physically, spiritually, emotionally. When God brings you out (and He will), you will be able to stand shoulder to shoulder to all of us who've been healed, delivered, and set free and shout at the top of your grateful voice, *"I am whole!"*

PICNIC

By Melanie Dees
Sumter, SC

"When the day came for the heavenly beings to appear before the Lord, Satan was there among them. The Lord asked him, "What have you been doing?" Satan answered, "I have been walking here and there, roaming around the earth." "Did you notice my servant Job?" the Lord asked. "There is no one on earth as faithful and good as he is. He worships me and is careful not to do anything evil." Satan replied, "Would Job worship you if he got nothing out of it? You have always protected him and his family and everything he owns. You bless everything he does, and you have given him enough cattle to fill the whole country. But now suppose you take away everything he has - he will curse you to your face!" "All right," the Lord said to Satan, "everything he has is in your power, but you must not hurt Job himself." So, Satan left!"
-Job 1:6–12 GNT

I have had the pleasure of attending several picnics in my life, and I am always amazed with the amount of food available. There are sweets— cakes, pies, cookies, homemade ice cream. Of course you can't forget the chicken, ribs, hot dogs, burgers, fish, corn on the cob, potato salad, and watermelon. There is every kind of drink, for both children and adults. Always included are those things that make a picnic specific to a culture. This event is always designed as an opportunity to have fun and fellowship. We look for a day when the weather will be perfect, and if we are near the water, that is an added benefit.

Since a picnic is held during summer, let's consider those things that are uninvited: flies, gnats, ants, rain, and hot weather, sometimes cats and dogs depending where the picnic is held. I have found that in the event that any of these uninvited guests attends, the picnic is rarely cancelled. God is teaching us how to trust him. There will always be situations we can't control or understand. If you refuse to leave the picnic because of the flies, don't leave God because of the test.

HUMPTY DUMPTY

By Michael Dempsey
Baltimore, MD

"Anyone who is joined to Christ is a new being; the old is gone, the new has come."
-2 Corinthians 5:17 GNT

I have realized that I have a lot in common with Humpty Dumpty.

Humpty Dumpty sat on a wall; I, too, sat on a wall of pride and selfishness, thinking I had it all. Humpty Dumpty had a great fall. I, too, had a great fall to drugs, alcohol, no self-esteem, and purposeless life. Nobody could put me back together. But Jesus came by and picked up the pieces, saved me, put me back together. Now I'm stronger, wiser, and better. I am now a new creature in Christ, from drug addict to preacher.

God is awesome!

MIRRORS DON'T LIE

By John R. Faison, Sr.
Petersburg, VA

"If you listen to the word, but do not put it into practice you are like people who look in a mirror and see themselves as they are. They take a good look at themselves and then go away and at once forget what they look like."
-James 1:23-24 GNT

Mirrors are a part of everyday life. Whether we are brushing our teeth, fixing our hair, or adjusting our clothes, we spend countless hours every year in front of a mirror, preparing to look our best. Perhaps women provide the best example of the power of the mirror, or at least that is what I gather from observing my wife. She is so in tune with the mirror that she keeps one with her at all times. Leaving the house without "checking herself out" is never an option. She, along with the rest of us, would never look into the mirror, see something wrong, and not do anything about it. That would be absolutely unthinkable. Right?

James tells us that the Word of God is like a mirror. Regardless of how often we look at it, it does exactly what it is supposed to do: it shows us as we truly are. It clearly displays our righteousness and our sins, our strengths and our weaknesses. Yet, an amazing phenomenon often occurs when we look into this mirror. After seeing the problems, we turn away from it as if nothing is wrong. We go about our days with messy spirits, even after the mirror revealed to us that we were untidy. Question: if we would never allow our physical appearances to remain unkempt, then why don't we exhibit the same concern for our spiritual appearances?

Today, take a relentless look in the spiritual mirror. If you see something that needs to be fixed, don't leave as if it does not exist. Denying it does not make it go away. Simply acknowledge what the mirror shows, and then let God groom you. The process will be revealing; the more time you spend in His mirror, the more you will begin looking like His Son.

DETERMINED TO BE LIKE JESUS

By Stacie Forrest
Ellicott City, MD

"All of us, then, reflect the glory of the Lord with uncovered faces; and that same glory, coming from the Lord, who is the Spirit, transforms us into his likeness in an ever greater degree of glory."
-2 Corinthians 3:18 GNT

A Tall Order

It's more than being kind and compassionate, honest and trustworthy. It's more than praying for our neighbors, giving our treasures, and helping the homeless. It's even more than witnessing, more than the worship on Sunday mornings, and more than the assurances we learn in discipleship. Singing a hymn, reading a scripture, and reciting the New Psalmist covenant may get us close to becoming like Jesus, but not close enough.

Jesus Christ was perfect, a man without sin who was made in the image of God. He loved totally, forgave completely, and healed absolutely. He was loved, and he was hated, but his entire life became ministry, devoting his existence to the Kingdom of God, and believing wholeheartedly in the salvation of lost souls. He walked among the sinners who were hated, disgraced, talked about, and scorned, but it was amongst the company of the harshly judged and disrespected that he was most comfortable. Few of us can say the same.

In a world of standards that are seemingly too difficult to fulfill, we struggle with the right and wrong of the world and in the concept of just being a good person. The mistakes of our pasts will haunt us, as we learn to live with the consequences and move toward the lessons learned from our errors. But what will it take to be accepted in the beloved and to hear the words, "Well done, my good and faithful servant?" The only logical first step is to love the Lord your God with all of your heart, all of your soul, all of your strength, and all of your mind; and to love your neighbor as yourself (Luke 10:27).

Becoming like Jesus is the commitment and dedication to a lifelong goal, a lifestyle always within reach but never quite obtained. It's a mission, an ambition, a hope, and a promise to follow God, obey his word, and keep His commands. It is forgiving without questioning, loving without a reason, and giving before being asked. We want to be like Jesus, but do we really want to take on the world as he did? Are we able to forgive the impossible? Are we able to love those that we can't like? Are we willing to turn the other cheek when we're hurt?

Prayer
"Most wise and wonderful God, our sole purpose is to love you to serve you and to become more like your Son, Jesus. The shoes will always be too big for us to fill, but we thank you for least of all opportunities to serve a God who will teach us to live a life rich in mercy and abundant in grace. We want to be all that you have created us for, and we want even more to reflect your image in every step taken and in every word spoken, for we know that you will honor the commitment that we have made to not only know you, but to become more like you. Now, God, we thank you for our patience with us and for tirelessly loving us the way that you. Amen."

THE HOUSE OF FEAR

By Alexandria Hawkins
Richmond, VA

On one episode of the detective sitcom *Monk*, we meet Monk's brother, Ambrose. While Monk has dozens of phobias, Ambrose has a phobia that does not let him leave his house. While this is troublesome in general, it becomes even more problematic when someone tries to force him out of his house by setting it on fire. Monk, upon solving the case, realizes the culprit will go after Ambrose, and when he arrives at the burning house, Monk runs inside to rescue his brother. Ambrose initially refuses to leave the house and tells Monk to leave without him. Monk refuses and says he can't leave without him and that he needs him. Eventually they both get out, and Ambrose realizes it is all right to go outside, thus overcoming his fear.

What if Monk's fears had kept him from reaching out to his brother and going into the burning house? Or what if Ambrose had refused to leave, letting his fear of going outside take his life and potentially his brother's life? What about our fears? Do our fears keep us from doing things even if the result is destruction for ourselves or others? Even if our fears are not obvious to others, they can be paralyzing and harmful to us if we allow this. While some fear is natural to make us aware of potential dangers, God did not intend for our every thought and action to be colored by fear to the point that we cannot move.

As one who has battled fear all my life, I have come to realize that fear can creep in when you don't even realize it and taint every part of your thought process. It was not until I realized that fear had been factoring into my decisions that I could recognize the extent to which it was binding me. Like Ambrose, I was willing to let the fear win, sure that life would go on without me, and I was even willing to die in my fear. Yet God (and people he has surrounded me with) refused to let me die in that fear. They convinced me that I was loved and needed. They pushed me out of the burning house that would have killed my destiny. As I stood outside the house of fear that had held me captive, I could breathe for the first time, knowing that there is life and possibility outside of fear. Most importantly, I had to realize that fear was a choice, and I could choose not to operate and act in fear.

So, if you are dealing with fears that grip and incapacitate you, then STAND:

Seek God—God's face, God's truth, God's promises, and God's heart for you.
Take God's love and wrap yourself in it, knowing that God's love and care are unconditional.
Acknowledge that God sees you as beautiful and with a purpose and that you should do the same.
Navigate your thought processes intentionally, refusing to let fear remain or shape your thoughts.
Devote your heart and mind to trusting God as God walks with you and guides your steps.

Trust is the fruit of a relationship in which you know you are loved.
—*Wm. Paul Young*

STAY FOCUSED

By Minister NaTasha S. Heath
Petersburg, VA

"Brethren, I count not myself to have apprehended: but this one thing I do, forgetting those things which are behind, and reaching forth unto those things which are before..."
-Philippians 3:13 KJV

Have you ever set goals in your life with every intention of fulfilling them? But, as life goes on, you find yourself not meeting the goals you've set? I want to encourage you to stay focused!

It does not matter if your goal is a natural or spiritual goal, God will help you meet it. Apostle Paul said to forget what is behind and reach for things that are before. In order words, don't let your past stop you from embracing your future. You may be asking, how can I stay focused? Here are some things you can do to keep focused:

- **Seek God first**: Matthew 6:33 KJV says, "But seek ye first the kingdom of God, and his righteousness; and all these things shall be added unto you." Seeking God first means before anything else is done, you ask God, "What shall I do?" and "How shall I go about this?" It's important to seek God to ask how to bring the goal to completion.
- **Pray:** Prayer is important because this is where you receive your direction from God on how to accomplish your goals.
- **Make a list**: Make a list of your goals, and separate the long-term goals from the short-term goals. As you complete them, check them off your list.

My brothers and sisters, I just want to encourage you to keep focused. Don't let your past hurts, disappointments, situations, and circumstances hinder the next level God has for you! God is with you every step of the way. You may have some difficult times, but be encouraged because the best is yet to come!

WATCHING MY SONS READ THEIR BIBLES

By Melody Patterson Jackson
Jacksonville, FL

A precious gift for me has not been an emerald, diamond, or jade jewel. It has been watching my three sons reading their Bibles. My daughter is still the reigning reading champ out of all of us, but my sons are catching up! As youngsters, a part of their punishment was reading Proverbs and The Chronicles of Nadia. (Boy was I hated.) We also listened to the National Public Radio stations wherever we lived. Our dinner table has always been filled with broad-scale dialog.

Now, discussion, laughter, and tears flow as we reminisce. Standing next to them in worship ... oh, I count that a privilege. As a young mom, I made a lot of mistakes with them. But the one thing I did fervently was get up through the night pray and anoint each of my children. As they grew up, Lord began to whisper, "Let go. Let them do. Let them be." Holding fast to Proverbs 22:6, I obeyed Him. It is so hard, but I do what He instructs.

As *responsible* men, so much rests on my sons' shoulders. The world is not fair. But neither is favor. As they search for a good woman to understand *them*, they seem to really "get" God. Even when mistakes are made, they tend to run to Him first. So on my journey to wholeness, God reminds me daily that our struggles never end, but there are a few precious moments that make this living thing worthwhile.

Pastor R.J. Washington said, "Reading the Bible renews the mind." I am thankful that our God is so awesome that He gave His Word knowing the comfort it would bring to all of us, including my daughter and my three sons.

BE STEADFAST AND UNMOVABLE

By April Kelley-Hill
Richmond, VA

"Therefore, my beloved brethren, be ye steadfast, unmoveable, always abounding in the work of the Lord, forasmuch as ye know that your labour is not in vain in the Lord."
-1 Corinthian 15:58 KJV

I left home this morning running later than usual. Getting into the car, I noticed there was a mosquito on the window. Not wanting to get bitten; I rushed to get into the car and slammed the door shut. I looked out, and the mosquito was still on the glass. Slamming the door did not cause him to fall off or fly away. I proceeded out of my cul-de-sac and on to the main road that led to the highway. I looked over, and the mosquito was still there. I thought to myself. *Mosquitoes must have super stick-em on their feet.* This guy was holding on, and I was driving about thirty miles per hour.

As I approached the highway and merged onto it, I said, "Now we'll see what mosquitoes are really made of." I proceeded to merge into highway traffic, often driving a few miles over the posted speed limit (after all, I was late). After about three or four minutes, I forgot about the mosquito, and my thoughts moved on to other things. When I arrived at work, I got out of the car to go into the building, and there he was! The mosquito had been steadfast and unmovable. No matter what doors slammed in his face, no matter how rough and bumpy the road was, no matter what the current conditions in his life were, the mosquito held on.

If a mosquito that weighs about 2.5 milligrams can hold on the exterior of a moving vehicle and survive a fifteen mile journey, often at excessively high speeds, why can't I hold on through whatever is going on in my life? Jesus already paid it all; the only thing I have to do is *hold on.*

TESTING: DO NOT DISTURB!

By Yolanda Kendrick-Dugue
Pompano Beach, FL

"I say this because I know what I am planning for you," say the Lord.
"I have good plans for you, not plans to hurt you. I will give hope and
a good future."
-Jeremiah 29:11 NCV

One day as I paced around the classroom as a proctor during a session
of standardized testing, I noticed two signs posted on the door. They
read: "Testing: Quiet" and "Do Not Disturb." Immediately, the words
on the signs ministered to my spirit. At that moment, I discerned the
admonition of the Holy Spirit concerning my "test anxiety." The words
served as a gentle reminder that whatever I was going through was all
a part of the process. I needed to acknowledge God's love for me and
His platform for perfecting my faith.

I continued to walk around the room with misty eyes and a calming
reassurance, knowing that God was transforming my experiences into
edification, without interruption.

Therefore, as redeemed recipients of the Kingdom, we have to
understand the supreme authority of our Savior. Even our most trying
and traumatic experiences will challenge us to remain faith- focused
and quiet during "testing."

PRAYER
"Dear Heavenly Father, I thank you for loving me so much and hearing
my heart's cry. Sometimes I don't understand but I have confidence in
your headship of my life. Help me to pass the tests of your plan and
purpose, and keep me aligned with your perfect will. In Jesus' name,
Amen."

KEEP YOUR COOL
(WHEN IT'S GOING DOWN)

By Robert Lyons
Louisville, KY

"The LORD is my light and my salvation; whom shall I fear? The LORD is the strength of my life; of whom shall I be afraid? When the wicked, even mine enemies and my foes, came upon me to eat up my flesh, they stumbled and fell. Though an host should encamp against me, my heart shall not fear: though war should rise against me, in this will I be confident."
- Psalm 27:1–3 KJV

In the first fight between Liston and Ali, Liston refused to fight after the sixth round. He wasn't knocked silly, knocked down, or knocked out. However, Ali hit Liston so hard, so fast, and from so many different directions that Liston refused to fight! How many times has life come at you so hard and fast and from so many different directions to the point where you were tempted to give up, give out, or even give in to the pressures of life by using an ungodly form of relief? Well David reassures us in Psalm 27 that when life comes hard and fast, we can keep our confidence, cool, calm, and composure by remembering a few things:

1. **Your Godly perspective**. Remember who God is and what He can do—anything He wants and everything you need!

2. **Your sense of purpose**. God has somewhere and something for you to be. Do and say and trust me, you're not smart enough to mess up what God has planned. This keeps us from seeking other sources beside the true source of life.

3. **Your Godly poise** by making sure your *faith is firm*. As long as you have been walking with God, you are undefeated. As you continue to walk with God, you will remain undefeatable. Your *focus is fixed*. God supplies us with spiritual bifocals. When our enemies are all closing

in around us, we must continue to look to the hills for our help. We will see our Father and not our foes. *You never forget your fights.* David told King Saul, "I have killed lions and bears, and I will do the same to this heathen Philistine, who has defied the army of the living God." (I Sam. 17:36 GNT) That's how you keep your cool when you know it's going down!

JOURNEY INTO WHOLENESS

By Yvonne McKesson
Jacksonville, FL

What is wholeness? You think to yourself when your heart has been broken, will I ever love again? A mother is told that her child is dead. Will the hole that is created ever be filled? A wife says her last good-bye to her husband, either by death or divorce. She thinks, do I ever want to love again? You go into work and find that you no longer have a job. You think, what do I do now?

These human emotions trap us every day, but God says, "I will never leave you or forsake you. I am with you even until the end of the age." These powerful words should be the battle cry every day. In the paraphrased words of Psalm 23, even though I am lost, God is still with me. He lights my path and gives me a place to rest. When folk talk about me and I am hurt, he gives me a shoulder to lean on. When I am wrong he parents me with his righteous and loving hand. He blesses me when I don't see the blessing.

Wholeness is when you turn your face from the world and turn it to God. It doesn't mean every day is a great day. Every day is a good day because God loves you. Remember, we are but the dust that God created, and he creates the wind to blow it away. Look to the hills for your help; health; the soothing balm of Gilead; the comfort of unconditional love; and the repairman of all the leaks, cracks, and holes that life may present. Walk in the comfortable of the Almighty God, and know that you are not broken; you are whole and held in the arms of God.

WHAT GOD HAS FOR YOU, IT IS FOR YOU!!!

By JoAnn N. Payne
Redan, GA

A season of financial struggle may have you asking God to come through in a particular area of your life. Could you be found praying for your bills to be paid or a job to support your lifestyle? Have you become frustrated because a promise you've heard is not currently being seen? Your challenge at this time is not to see the promise manifested. It is to remain faithful to the One who is and always will be your provider.

This time of struggle is the time in which you must honor God for the promise. It is during this tight situation that you are to be strong in your faith and not be consumed by what your natural eyes see and your natural ears hear. Now is the time to transcend beyond the natural into the spirit realm. It is in this place you will receive! You will receive power, patience, provision, and strength.

You may have cried out to God, asking for things that you feel you need. After days, weeks, and years, you looked around to find that you still have not received those things. It is then you would ask yourself if you needed it in the first place. You see, God provides you everything you need and at the exact time. I can say with great confidence that you have everything you stand in need of.

Whatever God has for you, it is for you alone and no one else. You no longer need get frustrated. God does not renege on His promises. While you are waiting on the manifestation of His promises, glorify His name and remain faithful. Always remember what God has for you, it is for you and without a doubt, declare it and believe it. Receive what God has for you!

A NEW YOU

By Quadgiela Quarles
Talors, SC

"Create in me a clean heart, O God; and renew a right spirit within me."
-Psalm 51: 10 KJV

Have you ever woke up and wanted a new life? Time and time again I felt that way until I discover that God would make me over again. I felt like my life was a wreck until I became a born-again Christian. My past failures, setbacks, and disappointments were all reminders from the devil. The devil will have you thinking things that are not true. Your thoughts become words, your words become desires, your desires become actions, and your actions become habits. Your thoughts can cause you to live in a world you have created with your own mouth. Life and death is in the power of the tongue. Be positive and speak positive, regardless of what the devil has put in your mind. That's why the Bible said to be transformed by the renewing of your mind daily (Romans 12:2).

In order to become a *new* you, you have to be washed daily with the water of the Word (Ephesians 5:26). Therefore, be careful what you watch and what you listen to. Exposure is the key to change, so expose yourself to the Word of God daily. Once you expose yourself, the Holy Spirit will come live in you and become your tour guide for life! Your tour guide will lead you where God has destined you to be.

So today, trust God, and believe that He will take control of your life. That's what faith is, believing for the impossible to come to past. Already see yourself becoming a *new you*, so you can experience a new beginning in God!

PURPOSEFUL WOMAN

By Sophia Robinson
Winston-Salem, NC

I am very excited about what God is doing in the lives of women. As women of God, we need to have a welcoming spirit that embraces other women. Sharing information is the key to living and being a purposeful woman. Since time began, women have fought one another for men and positions. We as women should not add to the pain of other women.

As we look in Genesis, we see two women placed in a hurtful position by the laws of the society. Let's take a look at Sarah and Hagar. Sarah the wife of Abraham and Hagar the bondservant are two examples of women who were at odds with one another because of a man. Hagar was a woman who was easily put away. We should get vexed at the thought of another woman being used and allowing herself a few moments of intimacy. Women around the world are in a position of being the other woman and receiving moments of love. They don't realize that they need to love themselves and come into the knowledge that God loves them unconditionally. God loved us so much that He gave His only begotten Son. He made a covenant with us by the shedding of blood. Why can't we give of ourselves to make sure that each woman we encounter knows about the goodness of the Lord? They need to know that where we are now is not where we've always been. We are not perfect people; however, our role as women is to inform and direct them to the Perfected One.

When we get delivered, we must deliver others. Do not stand in your deliverance and then look down your nose at other women who have not crossed the bridge to deliverance or even caught a glimpse of what it could mean in their lives. We need to be a mirror that will reflect where they are in love, and we need to use the reflection to navigate them to the bridge and onto the shore of peace in the Lord. Do not leave anyone behind. We dare not state that deliverance is easy, but we will continue to pray you through the rough spots where you may fall. We will be there to ensure you do not wallow in that fall.

Read Jeremiah 1:5 and hear what sayeth the Lord. God has given gifts in preaching, teaching, healing, deliverance, missions, outreach, singing, writing, design, musicians, business owners, etc. Use the gifts that are inside you. Some are lying dormant and can only be opened if that one person who has come through the storm you're currently in stands up and testifies how they made it to see a new day. Women of God, let us not be judgmental. We all had to start somewhere. Remember where you once were, and declare that you never want a young woman to go through that. Come on, women of God, let's band together. Bring forth the wailing and mourning women. Stay with our sisters until they are set free and completely delivered, and watch their mourning turn into dancing.

When women begin to demonstrate how the scriptures are made applicable in their daily lives, then and only then will we be able reach other women. Becoming transparent is not easy, but if God could allow His only begotten Son to enter into a world where he was vulnerable to most people, then we should be able to let go and be touchable and welcoming to a lost soul or soul who is weary. Go ahead girl and walk out "who" you are in God.

ARE YOU SICK AND TIRED OF BEING SICK AND TIRED?

By Janice Tucker
Jacksonville, FL

"When hope is crushed, the heart is crushed but a wish come true fills you with joy."
-Proverbs 13:12 GNT

Toward the end of 2008, we all were made painfully aware of the state of the economy. Wall Street was in a panic, the stock market was down every day, and large companies were declaring that they were on the verge of bankruptcy, thus adding to the number of people unemployed. Home foreclosures were on the rise due to balloon interest rates and the loss of jobs. In general, people are stressed out! They are sick and tired of the way things are. What is the answer to all of this you may ask?

Hope!

The Bible describes faith as things *hoped* for (Hebrews 11:1). We must realize that faith and hope are intertwined, and we need both. Hope is a confident desire, a wish, a source of success, or the happy anticipation of good things. One of the things my pastor, Pastor Guns, has recited as a mantra to us is to "enjoy the journey." We have this life right now, enjoy it!

Hope helps us to endure life! We become visionaries of our own destinies when we take a serious look at ourselves and ask God to mold us and make us into better saints. When we become true disciples, we then move through life's situations by being hopeful. Admittedly, it is sometimes easy for us to look at our situations and declare that it's never going to change (another trick of the enemy), but we have been taught and know that in this life something is always changing. The seasons, the weather, our attitudes—everything changes except God. Malachi 3:6 tells us, "For I am the LORD, I do not change." So when things seem hard and the cards are stacked against you, seek Him who does not change to guide you through with *hope* and confidence in *Him*.

During one of our church fasts, we were instructed to read Romans 12. As I did this, I fell in love with verse 12 and believe if we apply it to our lives; we will definitely be the better for it: "Rejoicing in hope; patient in tribulation; continuing instant in prayer"

Instead of being sick and tired, let's try to be hopeful and happy in Jesus and put all of our troubles in the Master's hand.

LET THE WORD DO THE WORK!

By Veronica Wright
Richmond, VA

Life brings about many fears, failures, and false starts. Even so, life doesn't just stop by the side of the road and drop us off; it keeps moving forward with us in tow as passengers. However, we do not need to create or concoct thoughts in our own minds of what we would like our purposes to be or where we want our final destinations to be. We already have someone who has taken care of that for us before we were even born. We can, however, speak those things that we desire to have in our lives because Matthew 7:7 clearly tells us that we can: "Ask and it will be given unto us, seek and we will find; knock and the door will be opened to us." For we know that according to Proverbs 18:21 that both death and life are in the "power of the tongue." When we speak the Word, the Word works.

Mark 5 introduces us to Jairus, a synagogue ruler whose daughter is dying. He took it upon himself to go to Jesus for help because he knew that the Word could heal his daughter. John 1:1–2 (KJV) says, "In the beginning was the Word, and the Word was with God, and the Word was God. The same was in the beginning with God." Jesus, the Word (made flesh), did the work and raised Jairus' daughter from the dead because Jairus took it to the Word, told it to the Word, and trusted in the Word. We must always remember to just *let the Word do the work.*

ONE WOMAN'S JOURNEY TO WHOLENESS

Just Call Me Hannah
By Althea Jefferson
Orlando, FL

I was pregnant! Within one month of "trying," I got pregnant! I couldn't believe it. I was absolutely thrilled. I remember enjoying the next few weeks by purchasing baby books and trying to learn all that I could about what I was going to experience. I spent more time daydreaming than anything else; I told everyone we were expecting a baby!

By the time I was ten weeks along, I experienced some spotting, and I immediately imagined the worse. On the way to the hospital, my husband, Beau, and I saw more mothers and children than we could count. It seemed like God had arranged a special family parade just for us. It made me sad because it felt like a "good-bye." I already knew what was happening. Beau and I said very little, even as we waited for the doctor, but I knew that seeing all of those families and children on the way to the hospital had touched him as much as it had touched me. We did not find out that day, but I had miscarried the baby we were expecting.

I was devastated and my husband blamed himself. I resented the world and my anger boiled over into every aspect of my life. I felt hollow on the inside and felt like life was over. My husband decided he didn't want me to "go through this again" so, he wasn't willing to even try getting pregnant again. I felt despair and fantasized about "running away" from my traumatic life. I wallowed in self pity. I could not understand why the man that claimed to love me so much was killing me bit by bit. Beau had decided for both of us that we were never having a family. I felt like he had cut away a very vivid and beautiful dream. His decision left me in a deep, dark, endless tunnel; I lived a despairing nightmare all alone.

It was during this time, a time that I call my journey to wholeness that I delved into the story of Samuel. I was fascinated with his mother, Hannah. I could relate to her so well and felt like her story was written just for me! I didn't know if I should laugh or cry when I read the eighth verse of the first book of Samuel. Hannah's husband was speaking: "What's the matter, Hannah? Why aren't you eating? Why be so sad just because you have no children? You have me. Isn't that better than having ten sons?" Elkanah sounded just like my husband. He was clueless! He could not grasp the pain his wife was experiencing and had no idea that he was being so insensitive. The Bible doesn't mention Hannah's response to her husband's senseless statements, so I won't mention my response either!

What Hannah did and so did I, was pray. Her prayer was so powerful and her focus was so deep on God that a bystander believed she was drunk with wine. Like Hannah, I was so focused on God during my grief that I don't recall much of anything other than praying into the wee hours of the morning. I felt closer to God than I had in a long time. Hannah ultimately promised her firstborn to God if He would grant her prayers to become a mother (I Samuel 1:2-11).

In her special petition to God, Hannah poured her heart out to Him. Her prayer gave me more strength, and it reminded me that we can always trust God in every situation and that we should never be afraid to ask Him for what we truly want. Hannah honored her promise to God and gave her son, Samuel, back to Him. Her son went on to become one of the greatest men in the Bible.

Let's face it, it had to be difficult for Hannah to give up her child, especially after being infertile for so long. I was truly amazed at her strength and courage and, especially, her faith. I learned so much from Hannah during my months grieving the child I had lost. By honoring her promise to God, she helped me fully understand that when we honor our promises to Him, we (and others) are blessed by our obedience.

I made many promises to God, and I know that He ultimately gave me a son so that others could be blessed with his life. This small child that I have the honor to raise has helped me to grow as a person and as a Christian in so many ways. I see how others respond to him, and I know that God has special plans for him and those of us that are surrounded by him.

I also learned to have more compassion for others because of my miscarriage. Most people cannot understand why a woman becomes so attached to a child in only two or three months, but pregnancy is the most incredible thing one could ever experience. To have it snatched away so suddenly is devastating. The woman's body has already begun to change, even in just a few weeks. Post-partum depression has a great deal to do with the changes after a miscarriage; your maternal hormones are at work, and most people don't think this is possible because you didn't come home with a baby.

Now, I have more compassion for those that experience the loss of a family pet. I certainly have more compassion for people who have low self-esteem and who lack in self-confidence. I used to pity people in these situations, but now I know better. I never wanted anyone's pity. I only wanted their prayers and understanding. That is what I try to give to others that appear to be in need—in need of love, in need of understanding, in need of help, in need of encouragement, and in need of support.

KEEP YOUR HEAD UP

By C.J. Wimberly
Gaithersburg, MD

Life can be hard, and life can be cruel.
Life can be dirty, and some choose to live it without any rules.
But you can't live your life focused on negativity.
In one ear and out the other, just let it be.
You must take it to God so he can help you see.
Don't hide it, disguise it, or cover it like a clue
Because our heavenly Father wants to help you.
He loves you unconditionally with an open heart.
When you are down, get up and get ready for your new start.
Lift your head to the sky, and smile, don't frown.
Give God all the glory because you have been found.
It will be all right. Trust me, this is just a phase.
The best thing you can do is turn to the next page.
You can start over, work harder. You can get through your trials
as long as you remember to walk with Jesus on every mile.
You are not alone. Jesus is in every one of your steps.
Jesus is there to help guide you, to give you that extra help.
Keep your head up high, and walk with pride.
He is there with you, always right by your side.
Like Jeremiah 29:11 says,
"For I know the plans I have for you,
declares the Lord, plans to prosper you and not to harm you,
plans to give you hope and future."
Because this ain't a joke; this is the real deal.
You can keep your head up high and look to the hills.
Keep your head up high, high to the sky. Jesus is the one that you want
to try.
Jesus is available to walk with you all the way home, and
if you receive him in your life, you will never have to worry about being
alone ...

CPSIA information can be obtained at www.ICGtesting.com
Printed in the USA
241122LV00001B/6/P